HATLEY PARK

AN ILLUSTRATED ANTHOLOGY

Edited by Geoffrey Castle

Canadian Cataloguing in Publication Data

Main entry under title

HATLEY PARK

ISBN 0-9699451-0-8

1. Hatley Park (Victoria, B.C.) 2. Dunsmuir, James, 1851–1920—Homes and haunts—British Columbia—Victoria. 3. Victoria (B.C.)—Buildings, structures, etc.—History. I. Friends of Hatley Park Society.
FC3846.8H37H37 1995   971.1'2803   C95-910341-4
F1089.5.V6H37 1995

Published by
    The Friends of Hatley Park Society
    Hatley Park
    Colwood, B.C. V0S 1B0

Designed and typeset by
    Nori Graphics
    1750 Cedar Hill Cross Road
    Victoria, B.C. V8P 2R3

Printed in Canada by
    Kromar Printing Ltd.
    725 Portage Avenue
    Winnipeg, Manitoba
    R3G 0M8

Cover photo from RRMC Archives
    Photo Credit: Darren Oxner

The Friends of Hatley Park

Board of Directors

Commodore (Ret'd) William Draper,
Chairman, Commandant RRMC 1983/84

Dawn Aleknevicus

Sidney Allinson

John Bergbusch,
Mayor of the City of Colwood

Geoffrey Castle

Rear Admiral (Ret'd) John Charles,
Commandant RRMC 1954/57

Mary Charles

Dr. David Krauel,
Dean of Graduate Studies RRMC

Heather Wilks

Captain (N) David Bindernagel,
Ex-Officio, Commandant RRMC

Original Historical Committee

Geoffrey Castle, Chairman

Mary Charles

Vivienne Clarke

Pam Ellis

Claire Inkster

Heather Wilks

Contents

Foreword

April 1995

In 1987, the Friends of Hatley Park Society was registered in British Columbia as a non-profit organisation under the *Societies Act*. The purpose of the Society is to promote and encourage the preservation of Hatley Castle, together with the out-buildings, grounds and gardens which were part of James Dunsmuir's Hatley Park Estate. In the same year, the Government of Canada designated the castle as a Federal Heritage building and, in 1994, this status was confirmed by The Honourable Michel Dupuy, Minister of Canadian Heritage. The Friends of Hatley Park Society intends to promote understanding and appreciation — especially among Canadians — of the significance of this designation, and the role of Hatley Park in the development of future leaders in Canada.

The first part of *Hatley Park — An Illustrated Anthology* outlines the historical and social events from the early Coast Salish Indian habitation, through the Spanish explorers, to the modern farm estate laid out and managed by Dunsmuir. The second half describes life at Hatley Park during the Dunsmuir era.

These buildings and grounds provided the environment in which Royal Roads Military College developed into a first-class national university. For more than fifty years, young Canadians from every province have come together to meet the demands of a military and academic program, and to learn about each other.

At Christmas time, the cadets sang carols in the Great Hall of the castle, found year-round serenity in the magnificent gardens and woods, and graduated with lasting memories of this college, together with a desire to serve their country when and where required. The college years, from the Province of British Columbia for management. The Society plans to take an active interest in the provision of maintenance and security for the heritage buildings and surrounding gardens.

The Friends sincerely hope that readers of this anthology, and others, will visit Hatley Park and encourage the preservation of the heritage of this unique property for the enjoyment of future generations.

The Society is grateful to everyone who helped in making this book a reality.

David C. Lam
Lieutenant-Governor of British Columbia

Acknowledgements

The Friends of Hatley Park Society are most grateful for the assistance they have received from writers, publishers and individuals to enable this book to become a reality at this special time of the last graduation ceremony at Royal Roads Military College, in May, 1995.

It was most kind of the University of Victoria to give permission for the Friends to quote passages from *Men of British Columbia*, by the late Derek W. Pethick. We are also indebted to Professor Sydney W. (Toby) Jackman and his publisher, Morriss Printing Company Limited, for letting us include a substantial portion of the section on James Dunsmuir from his book *The Men at Cary Castle*.

We also appreciate Martin Segger and Sono Nis Press allowing us to quote liberally from *The Buildings of Samuel Maclure*. Excerpts from *The Dunsmuir Saga* by Terry Reksten, © 1991, published by Douglas & McIntyre, are reprinted by permission.

Another debt of gratitude is owed to the *Times-Colonist* for their kind permission to use *Colonist* articles by Ginnie Beardsley, the late James K. Nesbitt, and Duncan McTavish. The Friends wish to acknowledge all the help given by volunteers. They collected photographs and talked with people connected in some way with Hatley Park when the Dunsmuirs lived there; Vivienne Clarke provided information on the Chinese who worked at Hatley.

We are grateful to Barry F. King and James Dodd, artists who permitted the use of their drawings, and to the City of Colwood for permitting the use of their maps of the archaeological and land use aspects at Hatley. Other sources we wish to acknowledge are Bruce Davies of Craigdarroch Castle Museum Society, the British Columbia Archives and Records Service, the Victoria City Archives, Hallmark Society, CFB Esquimalt Museum and Archives, Marlene Smith of the Esquimalt Archives, as well as Claire Inkster and Kenneth Mackenzie of Royal

Roads Military College Library and Archives.

Many other people were most helpful, including Pep Groos, Janet McLaren, Ian Sherwin, Mona Hansen, Violet Perkins, Wayne Dunsmuir, Phil C. Simpson, A.P. Bugslag, Edie Catterall, Ken Leeming, B.D. Quinney, Royal Roads head gardener David S. Rutherford, and Simon Lawrence of the City of Colwood, as well as those who indicated a preference for anonymity. In regard to notes on Dola Cavendish's house, Dolaura, we thank former owner Pamela Ellis. Bill Glover provided information about Laura Dunsmuir and St. Andrew's Church, and Dr. Elizabeth Hyde of the Synod Archives, Christ Church Cathedral, helped, as did Jo MacGregor of the Heritage Tree Society.

Also much appreciated was the willingness of Dr. David Krauel to read the proofs as the work progressed.

We apologise most sincerely if we have neglected to acknowledge help given either directly or indirectly, or suggestions as to whom we might contact for further information. Last, but certainly not least, we would like to thank the commandants and staff at Royal Roads Military College who, over the past few years, have always been helpful to the Friends and made their tasks, particularly that of writing this book, worthwhile.

Introduction

The justification for a building to be designated as a heritage structure is based on several important criteria, such as the age of the building, its architectural style, how original the building is, the present condition, and the impact its owners had on the community and beyond, as well as the nature of the land and the present and future uses, to ensure upkeep and viability in the long run.

Essentially, this book, *Hatley Park — An Illustrated Anthology*, was conceived by the directors of the Friends of Hatley Park Society as a companion to the earlier book, *Royal Roads Military College 1940–1990 — A Pictorial Retrospect*, by Peter J.S. Dunnett, a professor at the College. Bearing in mind that the final graduation ceremonies will take place in May, 1995, the Friends have collected historical, architectural and Dunsmuir family information, newspaper reports, photographs, maps, plans and illustrations, as well as anecdotes relating to the Dunsmuir era at Hatley Park.

James Dunsmuir, once the wealthiest individual in British Columbia, inherited a fortune but preferred to avoid political and public life unless he thought it might help to preserve or further his business interests. Rather, he was dedicated to a quiet life, shared with his wife, Laura, and the ten children. He was happiest hunting, fishing, and cruising the local waters in his steam yacht, *Dolaura*.

After living opulently at Burleith on the Gorge for some years, James and Laura discovered enchanting beauty not far from the mouth of Colwood Creek and the Esquimalt Lagoon. Dunmsuir began to acquire a large amount of land on which to build his ideal home. James instructed Samuel Maclure, the eminent architect who was about to remodel Burleith, to prepare a design for Hatley Park. He was given a virtual free hand, with the proviso that he accommodate the diverse requirements of both James and Laura. Construction commenced in the winter of

1908, and the "castle" was ready for occupancy eighteen months later. Dunsmuir, who was serving as Lieutenant-Governor of British Columbia, resigned from office and moved to his new home in 1909.

It is almost futile to attempt to compare Hatley Park to Craigdarroch Castle, built by James' father, Robert, twenty years earlier. Contrasting the significant features of Victoria's two major historical buildings is interesting. Hatley is linear in profile, whereas Craigdarroch is vertical. Hatley is Tudoresque in style, while Craigdarroch is Scottish baronial with Jacobean elements. Hatley stands in 650 acres of waterfront property. Craigdarroch had twenty-seven acres before it was subdivided following the death of Robert's widow, Joan, in 1908.

It has been said that Hatley Castle ("castle" implies the residence, and "park" suggests the building and land) emulates features of the English Tudor manor house, Compton Wynyates, which dates back to 1485. The similarities are probably related to the fact that Maclure's assistant, Douglas James, surveyed Compton Wynyates when he was training to be an architect. With notes for guidance, he designed the three-and-one-half-foot wall thickness in the tower of Hatley Castle.

Ashford Castle, Co. Mayo, Ireland. Sir Arthur Edward Guinness, later Lord Ardilaun, had this baronial edifice built on the banks of Lough Corrib. It was completed in 1870 and is a monument to Ireland's brewing industry. The castle is now a first-class hotel. (G. Castle sketch)

Replicas of earlier castles, and substantial borrowings of form, style and features, have occurred from time to time. One fine well-known example is Ashford Castle at Cong in County Mayo, Ireland. It was built in 1870 for Sir Arthur Edward Guinness and represents the zenith of Irish Victorian neo-Gothicism. It is now an exclusive hotel.

To construct a 15th–16th-century "mock" manor house and to meet with the approval of both James and Laura Dunsmuir was no mean task. Perhaps it was more surprising that the project went relatively smoothly and swiftly.

The Dunsmuirs were not the first to occupy this lovely part of Colwood. It was a place of the Straits Salish peoples, and there are several middens and burial grounds which have been identified. Later, near the mouth of Colwood Creek, there used to be a sawmill and then a tannery. The original Hatley Park was an estate and working farm owned by Roland Stuart. It was here that the British Navy obtained their fresh water supplies, as there are several fresh-water springs on the property.

The Royal Roads foreshore is a sanctuary for local and migrant birds, and on the estate there are some heritage trees which are of special interest. Wildflowers and animals thrive at Hatley.

When Stuart's house, which stood near the northern boundary of Royal Roads Military College parade ground, burned in 1905, Dunsmuir purchased Hatley Park and undertook a major land assembly project of adjacent parcels.

By 1911, Dunsmuir had sold most of his business interests and was settling easily into the life of a country squire. Over the next few years, he added landscaping, ancillary buildings, and a conservatory modelled on the one at Kew Gardens in England. He was a great supporter of the game of golf. Having already made it possible in 1906 for Victoria Golf Club to acquire the Pemberton land in Oak Bay, he and an associate, Joseph A. Sayward, purchased some of the old Esquimalt Farm land and laid out the Colwood Golf and Country Club ("Royal" was prefixed after the Prince of Wales paid a visit to Victoria in 1931).

The loss of his son Jim ("Boy") in the sinking of *Lusitania* in 1915 devastated James. He gradually spent more and more time hunting and fishing. He died at his hunting lodge by the Cowichan

River in 1920. He was nearly 69.

Life at Hatley went on in Laura's capable hands as she assumed a similar role to her mother-in-law, Joan Dunsmuir, who, widowed in 1889, stayed on at Craigdarroch until she died. With the valuable help of her estate manager, John Graham, Laura Dunsmuir attempted to make the model farm pay. However, during the long years of economic depression in the thirties, Hatley was costing $15,000 a year to run at a time when $65 per month was a good salary.

When Laura died in 1937, the household effects were auctioned and the estate was offered for sale. There was little or no interest, as the house was too large and expensive to maintain. Hatley Park was eventually purchased by the Canadian Government in 1940 for $75,000, and a Naval Officer Training College was formed the following year. If Germany had invaded England during the Second World War, Hatley Park might have become an alternative home for the British Royal Family.

In retrospect, probably no owner could have maintained Hatley Park better over the last half-century than Royal Roads Military College. It may be some consolation to recall that its future viability was considered when it was taken over on the [verbal] understanding that the castle would always be an educational establishment, as Peter Dunnett has pointed out in his book on the College.

Geoffrey Castle
Chairman, Historical Committee
Friends of Hatley Park Society
January 12, 1995

BEFORE THE DUNSMUIRS

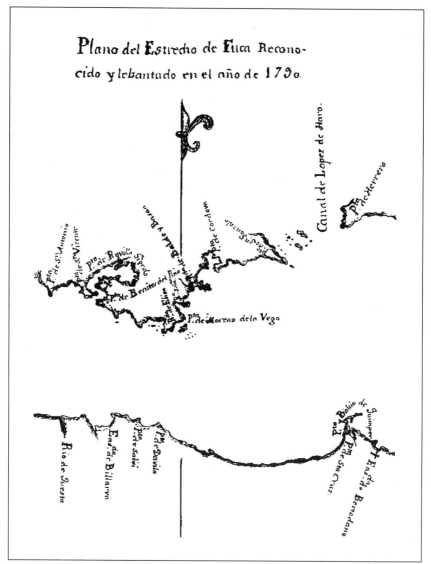

A portion of Quimper's chart, *Plano del Estrecho de Fuca Reconocido y lebantado en el ano de 1790*, showing Sooke Harbour, Royal Roads and Esquimalt Harbour (Puerto de Cordova). (BCARS Map Collection)

Before The Dunsmuirs

Dorothy Stranix

In 1789, the Spanish captured three British ships at Nootka. One of them, *Princess Royal*, was renamed *Princesa Real* and used the following year in the Spanish exploration of the Strait of Juan de Fuca, commanded by Manuel Quimper. [Ed.]

It is believed that Quimper left a record in the bark of a tree at Albert Head. An excerpt from his diary described his explorations along this coast:

"At three in the afternoon (June 30, 1790) I had the longboat and one of the canoes armed, and embarked with the pilot, taking along the

In June 1790, Manuel Quimper and Gonzalo Lopez de Haro (whom the English referred to as "Captain Arrow") entered the Strait of Juan de Fuca aboard *Princesa Real*, formerly the *Princess Royal* which the Spanish captured at Nootka. They anchored at Sooke and, at Royal Roads, where they went ashore, erected wooden crosses and claimed the land for Spain. Royal Roads was named Rada de Valdes y Bazan but was changed to Royal Bay in 1846. (Bob Banks sketch)

cross, for the purposes of taking possession of the farthest roadstead which I named [Rada de] Valdez y Bazan [changed to Royal Bay in 1846 and now Royal Roads]. At four in the afternoon I took possession, planted the cross, buried the bottle with all the other ceremonies with the instructions prescribed and fired repeated salutes."

The bottle was interred near a pine tree which was marked with a papal cross to identify it from others in the vicinity. The June 18, 1947 *Colonist* carried a story of a Douglas fir bearing axe marks which tallied with Quimper's description. It also notes that the fir tree was called a pine in the early days.

On January 11, 1794, the Spanish signed the third and last Nootka Convention. On March 28 the following year, final ceremonies took place as the Spanish flag at Nootka was replaced by the British flag. Then, in compliance with the terms of the Convention, the Spanish fort was dismantled and the Spanish garrison returned to Mexico. [Ed.]

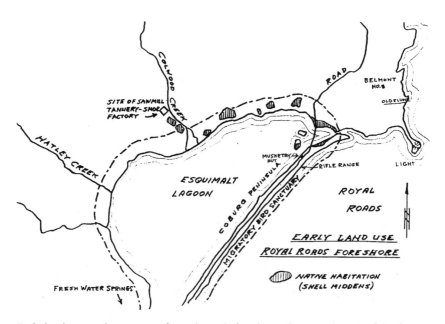

Early land use in the vicinity of Royal Roads foreshore, showing the site of the former Belmont sawmill, tannery and other features. Archaeological sites and migratory bird sanctuary area have been added. Based on a portion of one of a series of six map sheets compiled by the War Department, dated 1887. (BCARS)

In 1843, Fort Victoria was established. It was from this British out-post that the seeds of settlement spread to Metchosin, Langford, Happy Valley, Glen Lake and Colwood. Under a colonization agreement [between the Hudson's Bay Company and the British government] Captain Walter Colquhoun Grant became the first independent settler to come to Van-couver Island. His servants arrived in Victoria in June 1849. When Grant arrived, he decided to locate in Sooke. Although he stayed five years, much of the time was spent in exploring markets for forest products.

Meantime, negotiations with Indian tribes were taking place for land around Victoria. Compensation was given, but the Indians retained certain hunting and fishing rights. Metchosin was purchased from a decimated tribe of Coast Salish Indians.

On May 10, 1851, the sailing ship *Tory* brought the first English family to the Fort. The London office of the Puget's Sound Agricultural Company, a subsidiary of the Hudson's Bay Company, had chosen Captain Edward E. Langford to manage one of the four company farms. He was a retired officer of the Black Watch and owner of a 200-acre estate in Sussex. He was accompanied by his wife, Flora, and their five daughters. Shortly after their arrival a son was born. He was [believed to be] the first white male child born in the colony.

Langford took over the supervision of the 600-acre Esquimalt Farm, whose boundaries ran from Paterson Point, due south of Cole Island, to the northeast corner of the present Hatley Park estate. The farm house was called Colwood after Langford's Sussex residence. He was not a successful administrator, and spent a great deal of money, much of it for entertainment [especially visiting British naval officers], and the farm produced less than the owners would have liked.

Judge and Mrs. David Cameron resided at Belmont [now Fort Rodd National Historic Park]. Mrs. Cameron, sister of Sir James Douglas, was a second mother to the little Douglas girls who attended Miss Langford's Academy for Young Ladies. The Cameron home was a hospitable centre for ship's officers. When Mrs. Cameron died in 1858, naval men brought the casket from Belmont and carried it to the cathedral.

The Indians had looked with favour on the property which eventually became the Hatley Park estate, for it contained a burial ground where the Indians placed their dead in boxes and hung them in the trees. Another part of this land contained a sawmill operated by John Gilmore. According to one pioneer, the logs used to be hauled to the mill by oxen along a skid road which led from Sooke Road through the woods to the lagoon. So the mill provided work and lumber for the residents of the area from 1863. In the early 1870s the mill was turned into a combined tannery and shoe factory. It was managed by Mr. Switzer, who was held in high esteem by his employees.

The Muir brothers [the Muirs purchased the Grant property] brought hemlock bark from Sooke to be used in the tannery. Muir Creek was the source of most of this bark that was hauled by scows to Esquimalt. There it was transferred to Indian canoes and taken to the tannery. Every year about 400 tons of it were ground and used to tan the leather. The Indians not only had homes in the area, but employment too. Later, oak bark was imported from California.

Part of the land comprising Hatley Park estate contained a burial ground where the Indians placed their dead in boxes and hung them in the trees. (J.L. Vallance sketch)

A Trip to Hatley Park was an Adventure

Duncan McTavish

In the early 1900s, it was quite a trip from Victoria to Hatley Park to pay a visit to Roland Stuart, who was the owner of the property at that time. In company with my uncle, Harry Helmcken, we would board a tram car at Government and Yates Street, proceeding from there down Johnson Street, which at that time was a very popular business district.

On the corner of Store and Johnson was the Queen's Hotel, which was run by J.C. Voss, who later sailed around the world in his ancient dug-out canoe *Tillikum*, now preserved [in the Maritime Museum of British Columbia]. From here we would go along Store Street past the E & N Railway station, Albion Ironworks and Sayward's Mill, to the old Rock Bay bridge which the trams used until Bay Street was completed. Then on over the old Point Ellice Bridge which, tragically, collapsed through carrying an overloaded tram car during May 24th celebrations in 1896. Carrying on from there to the Canteen grounds, we might leave the tram car and proceed to Foster's pier, where we would take a launch with Sammy Doncaster as skipper, and so on across the harbour. Or, at other times we might take the tram car to the end of the line, walk through Esquimalt village — which was really a village then — and take John Day's launch to cross the harbour.

Aboard Sammy Doncaster's launch we passed Bullen's Marine Ways (later Yarrow's) and across the harbour at Constance Cove saw the old Hudson's Bay warehouse, where now stands the government graving dock. On landing at Rosebank, which belonged to my uncle, we would have lunch at Rosebank House with the caretaker, and then call on Mr. and Mrs. John Raymond, who operated the famous Rosebank Lime Kilns, a property operating under lease from my uncle.

Uncle Harry owned several hundred acres of the Rosebank land, which extended as far as Belmont Road. Adjoining his property was the old Belmont property, beyond which was Hatley Park. On leaving Rosebank we would walk up the trail adjoining Belmont to Belmont Road, which was the boundary, and, crossing the road, would take the trail through the woods and cross the stream, an area we called Ravensdale, and on which there was a very beautiful fall, which we knew as "The Sprite of Ravensdale".

After crossing the stream, we usually stopped to look at the old tannery, which stood at the end of the stream and was operated by a big water wheel. Carrying on from there, we would call on our friend, Roland Stuart, at his home at Hatley Park, and spend an hour or two with him. Hatley Park was then, as now, a very beautiful place, and often off Royal Roads we would see several sailing ships riding at anchor.

Mr. Stuart used to supply the navy ships with fresh water, which was obtained from a spring on the property, then piped from there to Belmont, and then from there to his water-carrying boat, the *Water Lily*, and delivered to the ships lying in Esquimalt Harbour. Mr. Stuart had this contract for a number of years, but before it was given to him, samples of the water were sent to London for analysis and found absolutely pure and fit for navy use. He had considerable land under cultivation and raised a lot of livestock, including horses, cattle and sheep.

Albert Bannister worked for him, taking full charge of the farm and water supply for the navy. Mr. Stuart was an old friend of our family. He was always a gracious host, making a visit to his home a great pleasure for his many friends. After visiting with him for some time, we would wend our way back to Rosebank and thence across the harbour at sunset, by launch as prearranged, and then home to Victoria by the old-time tram cars.

A day of interest, beauty, and pleasures of which I never tired.

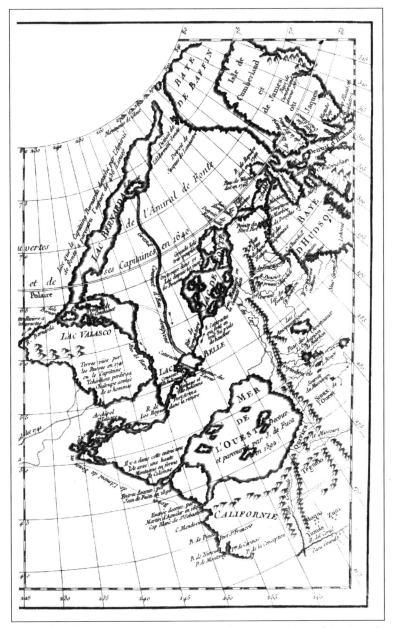

A map dated September, 1752, showing the discoveries to date of the Spanish, French, English and Russians, in particular those of Admiral de Fonte. The purpose was to find a northwest passage. Note that what is now British Columbia is shown as the western sea. (BCARS Map Collection)

Evidence of rough seas and stormy weather on and around this plaque, erected by the Thermopylae Club of Victoria, reinforces the words describing the fate of four vessels anchored in Royal Roads in April, 1863. (G. Castle photo)

Roland Stuart's house at Hatley Park, ca. 1893. (BCARS B-6328)

Haying time at Hatley Park, ca. 1900. L to R: Roland Stuart, Edward Conway and others, including Albert Bannister, Stuart's manager. Between the large trees and in the distance is Stuart's house and additions ca. 1900. (William Conway Collection, EA V987.20.10 N151)

Roland Stuart in 1931.
James Dunsmuir paid him
$50,000 in 1907 for 250 acres
comprising Stuart's Hatley Park.
(BCARS B-9645)

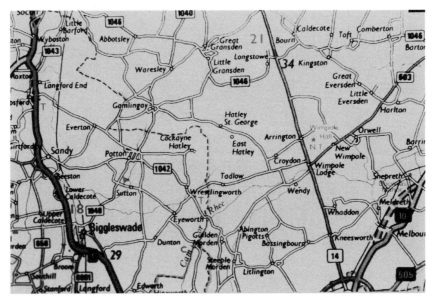

The origin of the name Hatley Park is intruiguing and subject to further research. There are three Hatleys between Biggleswade and Cambridge, in England — Cockayne Hatley, Hatley St. George, and East Hatley. (Source: National Trust)

THE DUNSMUIRS

Robert Dunsmuir — British Columbia's first Millionaire

Derek Pethick

The founder of the family fortune which eventually enabled his son, James, to build Hatley Castle, was Robert Dunsmuir. He was born in Hurlford, Scotland, in 1825, and received his education at nearby Kilmarnock. His father had been an overseer of coal mining operations in the area. Robert was orphaned at an early age and was brought up by Boyd Gilmour, an uncle. He married Joan Olive White in 1847, and, when Gilmour decided to find his fortune in the New World, Dunsmuir said that he would accompany him. The men contracted with the Hudson's Bay Company to assist in its coal-mining venture at Fort Rupert on the northeast coast of Vancouver Island.

Dunsmuir's wife needed some persuasion, as there were two children, Elizabeth and Agnes, and she was expecting another child, but, doubtless on the promise that he would some day build his wife a castle (Craigdarroch Castle was not completed until after the death of Robert Dunsmuir in 1889), the family embarked on the long voyage around Cape Horn. The journey almost ended in disaster when their ship, the *Pekin*, grounded at the mouth of the Columbia River. The crew took the opportunity to head for the California gold rush, and the Dunsmuirs made their own way to Fort Vancouver, farther up the river. That was where, in July 1851, their first son, James, was born.

Another vessel, the *Mary Dare*, took the party to Fort Rupert, where the family lived in a log cabin with bunks along the walls and an iron stove for cooking and heating. Water was carried from a nearby stream. At night the gate of the surrounding palisade was locked, and the guard would fire his gun from time to time. In daytime the Indians would come and barter furs.

It appears that, because they had never seen a fair-haired child before, some Indian women abducted the infant, offered a great many furs, and wanted him for their future chief. Dunsmuir was prophetic when he explained that his son would one day be a chief of his own people. (James later became premier, followed by his appointment as Lieutenant-Governor of British Columbia.)

It must have been a great relief to Mrs. Dunsmuir when, in 1854, her husband was transferred to Nanaimo. After his term of service with the Hudson's Bay Company expired, he took employment with the Harewood mine, also near Nanaimo. Meanwhile, the family continued to grow. There was another son, Alexander, and ultimately there would be eight daughters.

One day in October 1869, an event occurred that would have a profound impact on Dunsmuir's life. He discovered a very rich seam of coal not far from the present-day B.C. Ferries terminal at Departure Bay. Dunsmuir realised that a fortune was to be made, but lacked the necessary capital. He managed to persuade some British naval officers stationed on the coast (including Admiral Farquhar, Captain Edgerton and Lieutenant Diggle) to help finance the new venture. It was a significant year in other respects. The Suez Canal was opened, while in Victoria the old Christ Church Cathedral, built in 1856, was destroyed by fire. A petition addressed to U.S. President Grant asked him to receive British Columbia into the American Union. (He was in Fort Vancouver when James Dunsmuir was born.)

The firm of Dunsmuir, Diggle and Company developed rapidly. San Francisco became the chief market for coal, and the business justified the purchase of several ships. Dunsmuir was soon able to buy out his partners, and in 1883 Diggle received nearly three quarters of a million dollars for the few thousand he had invested. With his two sons taking an active part in the business, Dunsmuir was secure as the Steam Age replaced that of sail. James had apprenticed to a machinist and gained practical experience in an iron works at Portland, Oregon. After receiving some academic training in Ontario, he attended college in Blacksburg, Virginia, which led to his meeting Laura Surles of North Carolina, whom he married in 1876. Alexander was in charge of the company's office in San Francisco.

One of the terms of British Columbia's entry into Canadian confederation in 1871 was the building of the Canadian Pacific Railway. As it neared completion, Dunsmuir conceived the idea of a railway up the eastern coast of Vancouver Island, from Esquimalt to Nanaimo. With some financial backing from a group of American railroad tycoons, construction commenced in 1884. The last spike was driven at Cliffside at Shawnigan Lake in 1886 by Sir John A. Macdonald, the Prime Minister of Canada.

Some idea of the impact Dunsmuir made on British Columbia may be had when, upon his death in 1889, schools and businesses closed for the funeral from the Presbyterian church. His burial was the most elaborate in the history of the province; the only comparable funeral was that of Governor Sir James Douglas in 1877. Columns in the newspaper were outlined in black, and even a fire engine was draped in black. His widow moved into the newly completed Craigdarroch Castle, which her husband promised her some forty years earlier. She lived on an upper floor and occasionally went for a drive in her carriage, drawn by four horses and accompanied by a coachman and a footman. As she went along, she would gesture graciously, and people felt as if they had seen Queen Victoria.

Robert Dunsmuir's will left the Esquimalt and Nanaimo Railway and the San Francisco operation to Alexander, and James inherited all the coal mining and shipping interests. Then, when his brother Alexander died on January 31, 1900, James ended up in control of all the Dunsmuir interests.

James had opened an important mining operation at Extension and was creating an instant town at Oyster Harbour as a shipping port. Since November in the previous year, the Boers had laid seige to Ladysmith in Natal State, but on March 1, 1900, news of the relief of the town by the British reached James. This prompted him to name his new community Ladysmith, which, incidentally, lies on the 49th Parallel. On June 15, James Dunsmuir became Premier of British Columbia. Here was a man who appeared to have truly arrived.

Craigdarroch Castle was completed in 1890, a short time after Robert Dunsmuir died. Joan, his widow, lived there until she died in 1908. Later, the land was subdivided. The house is a well-known landmark and is open to the public. (Barry F. King drawing)

James Dunsmuir

S. W. Jackman

The death of Alexander Dunsmuir was to cause James Dunsmuir many problems. The former's widow received an annuity, but the bulk of the estate went to James Dunsmuir himself. His mother, his sisters, and his late brother's stepdaughter were all to contest the will. After a series of lawsuits, with the concomitant unpleasant publicity, James Dunsmuir finally emerged the victor in 1906. The legal battles caused relations within the family to become very strained indeed, and Joan Dunsmuir and her son were never properly reconciled.

The political career of James Dunsmuir was somewhat humdrum. He was essentially non-partisan, and he saw himself more as a manager than as a politician. He did not much care for debate and was inclined to take his own line, whether it was expedient or not; often his decisions seemed to be the result more of the businessman rather than the man charged with the administration of government. He regarded the opposition with much the same displeasure that he reserved for labour unions.

If he did not care for his role, it is clear that his wife and family felt otherwise. They were naturally in the forefront in most social affairs in the provincial capital. Laura Dunsmuir was an excellent hostess, and she liked people. In many ways her abilities in the social sphere smoothed over difficulties that came from her husband's rather dour outlook.

The Dunsmuirs went to England for the coronation of King Edward VII. They had a splendid time being received by the best people in England. It was rumoured James Dunsmuir was in line to receive a knighthood. Certainly it would have been in the tradition of the time to have given him this reward, and why it did not occur is somewhat of a mystery. His wife would have vastly enjoyed being "Lady Dunsmuir", but perhaps he simply did not see that it would really add anything to his own status to be known as "Sir James".

He was able to leave politics at last in November 1902, and Edward

Gawler Prior took over the government. Dunsmuir was happy to return to his private affairs.

There was general pleasure when it was learned that James Dunsmuir had agreed to serve as Lieutenant-Governor of British Columbia. On May 26, 1906, he took the oath of office as the province's eighth such incumbent. His term ended some three-and-a-half years later. He was not much happier in this position than he had been in politics. Again, it was his wife and daughters who found it agreeable. There were the usual social engagements, but with a real difference. The Dunsmuirs had a large family, composed of two boys and eight daughters. Consequently many elegant teas, dances, musical afternoons and evenings were held, and picnics which were graced by the Dunsmuir girls. The boys were not so involved in these affairs. Robert, the elder son, was an intrepid traveller and was often away from home; indeed, he never really lived in Victoria once he grew up. James, or "Boy" as he was known, was really too young to be more than a spectator. Probably at no other time until the Nichols resided in Government House were the young and their activities so much a part of the social scene. (W.C. Nichol's commission lasted from 1920 until 1926.)

Laura Dunsmuir, James Dunsmuir's wife, was truly the queen of local society. She became *the* Mrs. Dunsmuir when her mother-in-law died while the Dunsmuirs were in office. The elder Mrs. Dunsmuir took no part in the varied activities of her son and daughter-in-law. The households were at best on formal terms as a consequence of the awful lawsuit [resulting from James' brother Alexander's will].

If James Dunsmuir had chafed while premier, he was probably even less easy as Lieutenant-Governor. He had many difficulties with his workmen, there being numerous strikes, and he adamantly declined to recognize unions, preferring to close down operations than to face what he considered to be dictation. Some people even went so far as to imply that he cared nothing for public opinion, preferring to go his own way in all matters. This was an over-simplification; he was interested in his business empire, which had come about through the industry of his father, his brother and himself. He did not intend all these efforts to be swept away. He had the typical view of management in those days — the men

33

should be content to have jobs at all, and it was not their place to demand anything.

Emancipation from all public life finally came on December 11, 1909, when Thomas Paterson became the new Lieutenant-Governor. Dunsmuir's term had been shorter than was customary, but he had only taken the post largely to please his wife. He had gratified her desire and could now retire gracefully.

Laura Dunsmuir

*Based on an original work by
Terry Reksten, abridged,
rewritten, and substantially
altered by Geoffrey Castle*

Her position in society meant a great deal to Laura Dunsmuir. From the moment she arrived on Vancouver Island she took pains to let everyone know that she was a member (though the connection was tenuous) of the distinguished Byrd family of Virginia. She christened her first daughter Sarah Byrd ("Byrdie"). When James purchased a Rockland area home and registered it in Laura's name, she was quick to rename the house Westover, after the Byrd estate in Virginia.

In addition, Laura went along with the assumption that her father was a member of North Carolina's planter aristocracy, possessed of thousands of acres and hundreds of slaves. In actuality Laura's father, William Bright Surles, had fewer than a dozen slaves working Elm Grove, his 300-acre farm, even before the Civil War devastated Southern fortunes.

James Dunsmuir had become acquainted with Surle's son, Hannibal, when both were students at the Virginia Agricultural and Mechanical College in Blacksburg. James Dunsmuir, who was studying mining engineering, talked about the coal mines his father owned and how he was his father's right-hand man. When it became apparent that James had become enamoured of Laura, William Surles encouraged the suit.

Eighteen-year-old Laura Miller Surles married James Dunsmuir on July 5, 1876 at the old Sardis Church near the family home. The couple honeymooned on the way to Vancouver Island.

Laura's first child, christened Robert William after his two grand-fathers, was born at Wellington, August 21, 1877. Three months later, she received word that her mother had died of consumption, so she travelled back to Elm Grove, soon to discover that she was expecting another child. Sarah Byrd was born in North Carolina.

A third child, Joan Olive White, (named for her grandmother), was born at Wellington on August 7, 1880. Later that year the family moved to Departure Bay to live in a new two-storey house built on the hillside.

It had eleven rooms and fourteen-foot-high ceilings. There were eight fireplaces, each decorated with imitation marble. During the eight years at Departure Bay, Joan died at age three and, three years later, in 1887, Alexander Lee died before his first birthday. But later, Laura would recall her years at Departure Bay as the happiest time in her life.

In 1889, James, Laura and the family moved to Victoria to live in Fairview, the Italianate style house that Robert Dunsmuir built on Menzies Street in James Bay. As it was too small for the large family, James acquired twenty waterfront acres on the Gorge, and architect John Teague was commissioned to prepare a lavish Queen Anne-style house. Access was by a gently curving drive, and it was set amongst croquet lawns and tennis courts. The ground floor boasted a drawing room, dining room and breakfast room, a billiard room and a smoking room. Wide stairs rose from the oak-panelled central hall to the bedrooms and the day and night nurseries on the second floor, and then on to the third floor and an observation tower that provided a view across the waters of the Gorge to where Emily (Robert Dunsmuir's daughter) lived at

James Dunsmuir and his family moved from Fairview on Menzies Street to Burleith, overlooking the Gorge, in 1892. This fine Queen Anne style mansion was designed by John Teague, who, in 1894, became Mayor of the City of Victoria. (G. Castle sketch)

Ashnola. "The house throughout will be lighted up by electricity, with electric bells, speaking tubes and every modern convenience," the *Colonist* reported. This was Burleith, named after Robert Dunsmuir's birthplace in Scotland.

Before the turn of the century, the Dunsmuirs were at the peak of Victoria society. Robert Dunsmuir's children's homes — Mount Adelaide, home of Mary and Henry Croft (now the site of Matson Lodge); Ashnola, residence of Emily and Captain C.P. Snowden (Gorge Road Hospital); Burleith, which was destroyed by fire some forty years after it was built in 1891 — set standards that none could match. Laura introduced James to the arts, and she succeeded in turning him into an "admirer of the drama, and an ardent lover of good music." In 1901 she took delivery of a Steinway parlour grand, the "most costly and beautiful piano ever imported to British Columbia," and began to hold recitals at Burleith.

The Dunsmuirs were noted for their fine homes. Ashnola was designed by Leonard Buttress Trimen. The house was a wedding gift, in 1888, from Robert Dunsmuir to his daughter, Emily, and her husband, Captain Northing Pinckney Snowden. It was located across the Gorge from where Burleith would be built later. The house was demolished in 1971 to faciliate an addition to Gorge Road hospital. (Barry F. King drawing)

Every winter she insisted that the family travel south to spend a month at San Francisco's Palace Hotel for the city's opera season.

The most notable people Laura hosted at Burleith were the Duke and Duchess of York (the future King George V and Queen Mary).

Laura's southern charm won her instant acceptance by all from the time of her marriage to James, who proved to be a fond and loving father. When Dola was born September 25, 1903, the seven other surviving children ranged from Robert (Robin), twenty-six years of age, down to nine-year-old James ("Boy"). Sarah Byrd ("Byrdie") was twenty-four and Elizabeth Maud had recently celebrated her twenty-first birthday. Then there was nineteen-year-old Laura Mary and fifteen-year-old Emily Elinor and her sister, Joan Marion, only one year younger. Jessie Muriel was thirteen and Kathleen was almost twelve.

THE FAMILY OF JAMES AND LAURA DUNSMUIR

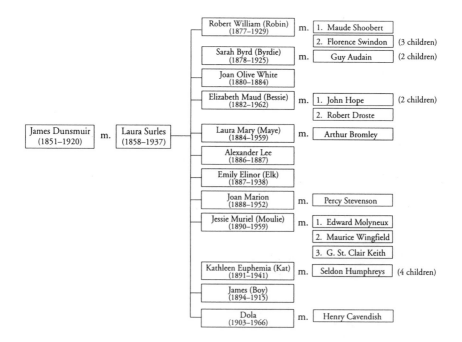

Robert Dunsmuir became the wealthiest individual in British Columbia. He and his wife, Joan, were the parents of two boys and eight girls. (RRMC)

Joan, wife of Robert Dunsmuir, finally got the castle her husband promised her when they left Scotland some forty years earlier. It was unfortunate that Robert died before Craigdarroch Castle was ready for occupancy. (PABC 2699)

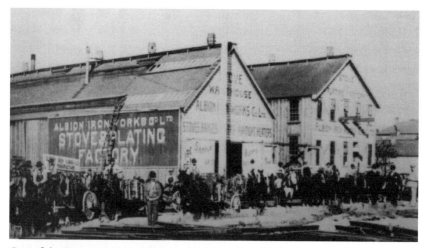

One of the Dunsmuir enterprises was the Albion Iron Works. It occupied three-and-one-half acres of land at Pembroke and Discovery streets. Shipbuilding, boiler making, and ironwork for commercial building construction were undertaken. Sixty thirty-ton rail cars were supplied to Dunsmuir's Esquimalt and Nanaimo Railway. In 1905 the company began manufacturing its famous stoves. (BCARS)

Fairview, James Dunsmuir's parents' first home in Victoria, was at the southwest corner of Menzies and Quebec streets. Since it was not large enough for James and Laura Dunsmuir's family and entertainment requirements, the architect John Teague was commissioned to design Burleith, on the Gorge. (CCA)

James Dunsmuir's support for golfing was significant. In 1906, he lent the Victoria Golf Club, in Oak Bay, money to purchase the land already under threat from development. Photo shows the club house around that time, with the roof recently raised to make more interior space. (Victoria Golf Club)

James Dunsmuir preferred hunting and fishing to expanding the family fortune and engaging in politics. He and his wife, Laura, had three sons and nine daughters. (RRMC)

Laura Dunsmuir exuded Southern charm and was very proud of her ancestral connection with the Byrds, a prominent American family. (RRMC)

At the Hunt Cup Races at Colwood in 1898. James Dunsmuir's sisters, Mary (Croft), Emily (Snowden) and, holding parasol, Jessie (Musgrave). The others are Martha (Barnard), Emma and Dolly. (Private Collection)

Dola on her horse, Beauty, taking one of her earliest rides. (RRMC)

Laura Dunsmuir was a wonderful hostess. The guest book from Hatley Castle is preserved in the B.C. Archives and Records Service. (RRMC)

Burleith ca. 1893 before additions. Family members on the porch and in the carriage. The architect was John Teague, who designed City Hall, Royal Jubilee Hospital, and part of St. Anne's Academy, among others. (BCARS A-8641)

Burleith and grounds. The children's playhouse is over on the left. (Private Collection)

Playhouse at Burleith with the Dunsmuir children ca. 1893. A little house was built later at Hatley Park for Dola. There was also one at Ellora for the Audain children and their friends. (Private Collection)

The little Dunsmuir girls, left to right: Elinor, Muriel, Marion and Kathleen, with "Way" lying in front. Photograph taken by Frank Barnard at his home, "Rockwood", in 1893. The Barnards moved from Rockwood, owned by the Loewens, to "Clovelly", below Esquimalt Road. Other friends and neighbours were the Pooleys. C.E. Pooley was the Dunsmuirs' lawyer. (Private Collection)

The family of James and Laura Dunsmuir around the time of the building of Hatley Castle. L to R: (back row) Robert (Robin) and wife, Maude; John Hope (married to Bessie), an unidentified friend or relative, Arthur Bromley (holding dog), his wife, Maye, and Guy Audain, husband of Byrdie. (centre row) Bessie, Laura and James, her husband; Boy is standing behind his parents; and Byrdie. (front row) Marion, Kathleen, Dola, Jimmy Audain, Elinor and Muriel. (BCARS H-2835)

Laura Mary (Maye), fourth daughter of James and Laura Dunsmuir. She married Arthur, the younger son of Sir Henry and Lady Bromley. Hers proved to be the best marriage of the Dunsmuir girls. (CCA)

Joan Marion, sixth daughter of James and Laura Dunsmuir. In 1913, she married Percy Stevenson in England, but he died suddenly nine years later. Marion never remarried. (CCA)

47

Sarah Byrd ("Byrdie"), who married Guy Audain, with her sister, Joan Marion. (CCA)

James Dunsmuir on the terrace of the newly completed Hatley Castle, ca. 1910. (BCARS H-2831)

The daughters of James and Laura Dunsmuir. Back row, L to R: Joan Marion, Laura Mary, Jessie Muriel and Kathleen. Front row, L to R: Dola Frances, Sara Byrd, Elizabeth Maud and Emily Elinor, at Hatley ca. 1913. (CCA)

James and Laura Dunsmuir, the Littles, Mrs. Joshua Freeman and other friends aboard *Dolaura*, ca. 1913. (CCA)

"Boy" astride his grey dapple "Kismet", ca. 1913. (Private Collection)

Jim ("Boy") Dunsmuir at Hatley Castle mounted on Kismet. This is one of the last photographs taken of Boy, in April 1915. He died in the sinking of the *Lusitania*, May 7. (BCARS ZZ95019)

In the courtyard of the stables, probably early spring, 1915. L to R: Pony Beauty, stableboy, Kismet and Nigger on either side of Boy, head groomsman W.E. Mann (holding horses), and other unidentified men and horses. (BCARS H-2837)

Another successful expedition aboard *Dolaura*, hunting and fishing. L to R: James Dunsmuir, Major Guy Audain, friend "Dib" Little, Dr. Taylor, and Mr. Burton. February 22, 1911. (BCARS ZZ95021)

Jimmy ("Boy") Dunsmuir.
All of James Dunsmuir's hopes
for the future of the family were
vested in this young man. (CCA)

Jimmy ("Boy") and "Nigger" taking a jump. (Private Collection)

Out for a ride. Dola and unidentified companion at the foot of the Neptune steps in the grounds of Hatley Park, ca. 1914. (CCA)

James in a happy mood.
He is aboard his yacht.
(BCARS H-2818)

HATLEY PARK

Preparations for a Change of Life Style

Based on an original work by Terry Reksten, abridged, rewritten, and substantially altered by Geoffrey Castle

When on November 21, 1902, James Dunsmuir resigned his Premiership, he was determined to simplify his life, not only by turning his back on politics, but also by selling the Esquimalt and Nanaimo Railway. His involvement in politics may have been of some benefit to his industrial interests but, almost more than anything he wanted to enjoy his wealth and his family.

Negotiations had broken down when potential purchasers, who were interested in acquiring the coal mines as well as the railway, were concerned about the promising future of the oil industry. Dunsmuir's American partners in the railway, also preferring to invest in oil, agreed to sell their interest to Dunsmuir for one million dollars. Three years later he sold the E & N to the Canadian Pacific Railway for $2,330,000. The CPR also gave land and right-of-way concessions to the Wellington Colliery Company of Dunsmuir and granted coal mining rights on all the land comprising the E & N right-of-way for the operation of the mines.

By May 1906, Dunsmuir was selected to replace retiring Lieutenant-Governor Henri Gustave Joly de Lotbiniere. The *Toronto-Globe* had predicted the outcome on the basis that the people of British Columbia wanted a Lieutenant-Governor of their own province, and, secondly, few prominent British Columbians were able to make the financial sacrifices of the Lieutenant-Governor. So the man who shunned public appearances and preferred the comforts of home and the pleasures of hunting and fishing was encouraged by his wife to accept one of the highest offices in the country.

A year later, when the B.C. Legislature passed "An Act to Regulate Immigration into British Columbia" designed to exclude the Japanese, Dunsmuir informed the premier that he would not give assent to the bill, particularly in view of the federal government having just concluded a trade agreement with Japan. Also, Dunsmuir wanted to import 500 Japanese coal miners for his collieries.

As other issues started to work against Dunsmuir, he began to prepare to leave Government House, although he could have continued until the summer of 1911. During the winter session of 1908, Dunsmuir was labelled as a brute, "an inhuman monster", "a champion union-basher", "an honourable scalawag".

Whenever he could, he boarded his yacht, *Thistle*, sailed away from his troubles in the company of undemanding friends (in truth, he was not a good sailor), and headed for his favourite hunting and fishing places such as Knight Inlet and the inlets and bays of the Queen Charlotte Islands.

Thistle was steaming through a quiet sea in Queen Charlotte Sound, and Dunsmuir and three companions were having lunch after bagging a dozen bears, four of which were grizzlies, when fire started in the engine room. The passengers, crew and Captain Bissett took to the lifeboats while the 116-foot-long vessel of 384 tons burned to the waterline. The captain thought that the cause of the fire was the spontaneous combustion of coal dust — the dread of many a coal miner. Afterwards, Dunsmuir said that his greatest regret was the loss of the bearskins.

Three months later, an order was placed with a builder on the Clyde for *Dolaura*. This magnificent steam yacht was built of steel and measured 218 feet in length with a beam of 32 feet. Its cruising speed was a respectable fourteen knots. The drawing room was twenty-four feet by eighteen feet and panelled in Spanish mahogany. Chairs were covered in pale blue silk brocade, and there was a large fireplace. The dining room could seat twenty-four people. The white-tiled bathroom had a Doulton tub, and the washbasins were of Venetian marble with silver fittings. There was also a library and a smoking room.

In March, 1908, Dunsmuir and his family went to Scotland to take delivery of *Dolaura* (named for Dola and Laura) and visited North Sea ports. They navigated the locks of the 100-kilometre-long Kiel Canal connecting the North Sea with the Baltic Sea. *Dolaura* came alongside the German emperor's yacht, *Hohenzollern*, and piqued the Kaiser's curiosity. He invited Dunsmuir aboard and the invitation was reciprocated.

Upon his return to British Columbia in August, 1908, Dunsmuir felt like a new man. Having put all thoughts of business out of his mind, he was looking forward to getting real enjoyment out of life and would soon divest himself of his mining interests.

It was with these thoughts continually running through his mind that James Dunsmuir had commissioned architect Samuel Maclure to rebuild Burleith, but a piece of land that fitted much better into Dunsmuir's retirement plans became available. Roland Stuart had decided to sell Hatley Park, his 250-acre estate on the Esquimalt Lagoon.

Gilzean Roland Whately Stuart had moved to Vancouver Island after twice failing to qualify for a crack English regiment. In 1892 he acquired title to 250 beautiful acres on the Esquimalt Lagoon, immediately west of the deep bay that was home to the naval station, and facing south across the Strait of Juan de Fuca for a breathtakingly unrestricted view of the Olympic Mountains. There, in a picturesque Tudor-style house with curtains of Battenburg lace, Stuart lived a gracious life, In 1902 his mother died, and after erecting a towering obelisk in her memory, he built a new wing on the house. In August 1905 the house burned down. Gone were the oil paintings, valuable antiques and his library, which

Roland Stuart's Hatley Park. The name may have come from England. The original house was enlarged in 1902 but was destroyed by fire three years later. (G. Castle sketch)

had contained manuscripts and a lengthy correspondence belonging to his mother's friend, Mary Ann Evans, the novelist George Eliot.

In 1907, Stuart having announced that he intended to leave the island for good, James Dunsmuir paid $50,000, took possession of Hatley Park, and announced that he planned to lay out a model estate. Maclure shelved his Burleith sketches and began working on the most important commission of his life.

In 1908 James added a second 250 acres, and after a third acquisition two years later, Hatley encompassed almost 800 acres. He spent $134,000 for the land. What the rest cost can only be imagined, for James was planning much more than just a fine house in the country. He saw himself as the lord of the manor, at the centre of a self-contained feudal village. There would be a model dairy and stable, both floored with rubberized bricks; a glass conservatory, capable of growing vegetables and fruits, including bananas, as well as Laura's white orchids; and Hatley would have its own slaughterhouse, smokehouse and refrigeration plant. Hidden in the trees, a discreet remove from the main house, would be a Chinatown large enough to accommodate the labourers required to weed the gardens, thresh the grain, collect the eggs, milk the cows, harvest the crops and to turn Hatley into a working farm and a paying proposition. Hatley's wooded acres would be stocked with game so that James Dunsmuir could invite his friends to come for country-house weekends of shooting and hunting.

BUILDING HATLEY CASTLE

The Architect

Martin Segger

Samuel Maclure was born on April 11, 1860, at the Royal Engineers' camp at Sapperton. He had the honour of being the first white child whose birth was registered in the colonial capital of New Westminster. His father, John Cunningham Maclure, was born in Wigtownshire in Scotland, in 1831. He came to British Columbia with the Royal Engineers, commanded by Colonel Moody, in 1858. He had trained as a surveyor and, while engaged in the first major trigonometrical survey of the British Isles, met and married Martha McIntyre, in Belfast. They moved from Sapperton to Hazelbrae in 1868, where they raised their family of three boys and two girls.

John Maclure surveyed for the abortive Collins Overland Telegraph line which would link North America and Europe by cable via British Columbia, Alaska, the Bering Straits and Russia. The line was abandoned when the Transatlantic cable was successfully completed in 1868. However, John had become an expert telegrapher. This was to prove useful when the Maclure home became the Matsqui repeater station for the U.S. – New Westminster section of the transcontinental cable. All the children became proficient key operators. Furthermore, the family acquired conversational "Chinook", learned from the local Indians.

All the children did well by their upbringing. Sarah married J.C. McLagan, manager of the *Victoria Times* who, in 1888, founded the Vancouver *World*. When her husband died, Sarah became editor and managed the paper. Susan married William McColl, stepson of another Royal Engineer, while Fred and Charles later founded British Columbia's largest brick factory at Clayburn, near Abbotsford.

Sam Maclure, the oldest son, attended Boys' Central School in Victoria for a time. At an early age he began to emulate his father's interest in nature and would sketch and paint. His parents encouraged him, but a family financial setback caused Samuel Maclure to return home and operate the telegraph station. His numerous subsequent stations were noted for their profusion of floral displays and window boxes of nasturtiums which he cultivated with great devotion. He was eventually able to achieve his ambition and devote a year to the formal study of art in 1884. He was twenty-four.

He attended the Spring Garden Institute in Philadelphia, toured art galleries and visited Boston, New York and other cities. Founded in 1850 as one of the pioneer technical training schools, architectural and mechanical drawing were part of the early curriculum, and by 1878 drawing classes had developed into regular art classes. Other subjects were steam engineering, plumbing, wood and metal work. Rapid industrial and commercial expansion heralded a new wave of architecture, and when Maclure returned home he was determined to turn his artistic talents to the practice of architecture.

For a while he worked for the Esquimalt and Nanaimo Railway as a telegraph operator while studying building construction, design and architectural history. It was during this time that he met Miss Margaret Catherine Simpson, stepdaughter of the Reverend Patrick MacFarlane Macleod, rector of St. Andrew's Presbyterian Church in Victoria. The couple met at church. She was a talented musician and devotee of the arts. Because of Maclure's lack of prospects for the future, Margaret's family discouraged thoughts of marriage.

Maclure opened his architectural practice in New Westminster in partnership with Charles Henry Clow and shortly received a substantial commission — the new public hospital in New Westminster. Samuel was twenty-nine and planned, together with Sarah, to elope with Margaret. The Macleods became suspicious when Margaret failed to appear for dinner. They searched the town, and Margaret's brother was sent to watch the ship sailing for the mainland that night. Nobody noticed a bent, shabbily dressed old woman as she hobbled along the gangplank. Margaret's disguise was successful, and the marriage took place in a quiet ceremony at the McLagan home in Vancouver.

The Temple Building (525 Fort Street) commission from family friend Robert Ward was to prove crucial in establishing Maclure's Victoria practice. Ward was an archetypal new world entrepreneur. No doubt

Maclure's success with the company's head office building prompted further commissions. Of particular significance, however, to the Robert Ward association was the fact that Robert's brother William was managing director of the Bank of British Columbia. This powerful institution, feared and revered by businessmen and politicians alike, fronted for British backers who financed not only the colony and later the province, but for most of British Columbia's major business interests. A major shareholder and director of the bank was coal magnate and financier James Dunsmuir, by far the wealthiest man in the province.

The first Dunsmuir commission (Allingham) was James' wedding gift to his son Robin. This house, overlooking Esquimalt Harbour, was built in 1900. Similar commissions followed in short succession. The crucial commission was, however, the one for the new Government House to replace the former structure which burned completely in 1899. (It was home for the Dunsmuirs from 1906 to 1909).

The Temple Building, on Fort Street, was built in 1893. It is one of Samuel Maclure's few commercial examples, but the commission gained the architect some wealthy clients, such as the Dunsmuirs. The building is now the home of Victoria Chamber of Commerce. (Barry F. King drawing)

The Esquimalt and Nanaimo Railway was owned by the Dunsmuirs, and later it was bought by the Canadian Pacific Railway. Banker to the CPR was the Bank of Montreal, from which Maclure received a number of commissions. Robert Ward, as a well-connected businessman and sometime magistrate, may also have provided an introduction to Victoria's legal circles, such as the 1899 commission from Judge Albert Edward McPhillips, and in 1904 from Alexis Martin, both in the Rockland area.

James and his wife were no doubt impressed with the superbly crafted elegance of Maclure's Cary Castle (Government House) interiors and had probably settled on him as architect for their new home (Hatley), but it was Robin who suggested an English-country-seat design based on the sixteenth-century Warwickshire manor house, Compton Wynyates. [Wynyates is Old English for "windy valley".]

Compton Wynyates embodied the essence of what the English Elizabethan and Queen Anne revivalists sought in the rambling plans and detailing of their new commissions. It was common for these English architects to draw their detailing directly from archaeological field trips.

Maclure, a shy, often retiring man of frail health and wry humour, though busy, accepted the commission. While Hatley Park would be the

Compton Wynyates was constructed over a period of forty-eight years, starting in 1480. Hatley Castle incorporates architectural features evident in this Elizabethan Warwickshire manor house. (G. Castle sketch)

product of Maclure's artistic imagination and experience, it is fascinating to study how much of Compton Wynyates is embedded in the Hatley Park scheme. To assist him in the huge project, which called for some 248 drawings, Maclure obtained the services of Douglas James, a young Englishman who, as part of his training, had spent time sketching and measuring historic country houses, one of them Compton Wynyates.

The Dunsmuir castle is the skin of Wynyates with many of its elements re-arranged, wrapped around a totally different plan — the tall castellated tower block and commodious entrance porch, the half-timbered and bargeboard gable ends, banks of stone mullioned windows, end towers, faceted Tudor chimney stacks, and crenellated parapets, repeated but reorganized in Hatley Park. The symmetrical proportions and the balanced harmony of quarried granite massing in Maclure's work replaces the rambling nature of the English manor brickwork and masonry forms. In substance, the spirit of the two structures have little in common. It should be noted that Compton Wynyates is some 400 years older than Hatley Park.

The choice of the location seems to have been Mrs. Dunsmuir's, and it was she in particular who was attracted by the woodland setting, swards of open meadowland, and the delightful glen with its sun-drenched waterfalls and towering crooked arbutus trees adjacent to which the house was built. The property sloped gently down to the sea-shore and a large, crescent-shaped lagoon where visiting launches could shelter, and the family steam yacht, *Dolaura*, might be anchored offshore.

Beginning in 1908, the design and construction process assumed the normal pattern of Maclure's close client, architect and trades relationship, except on a much vaster scale. James Dunsmuir approved the overall scheme and the final designs, but the details, from the first concept to the interior decorations and furnishings, involved close collaboration with James' wife, Laura. The plan of the Hatley residence is a near duplicate of Cary Castle, although without the central wing containing the public ballroom. A large porte-cochere would shelter the main entrance on the north side. It is interesting to note that just before Dunsmuir retired as Lieutenant-Governor in 1909, he asked F.M. Rattenbury to design a similar feature for Government House. The cost was $3,429, and today it is the only remaining part of the great house, which burned completely in 1957.

Porte-cochere at Government House was added by Lieutenant-Governor James Dunsmuir in 1909 for a cost of $3,429. The structure survived the 1957 fire which razed the house. It was incorporated into the new vice-regal mansion. (Barry F. King drawing)

Samuel Maclure, son of one of the Royal Engineers who came to British Columbia in 1858, is believed to be the first white child born in New Westminster. Hatley Castle was probably the most significant commission in his brilliant forty-year architectural career, which lasted until 1929. (Courtesy Vancouver City Archives)

Samuel Maclure and Francis Mawson Rattenbury collaborated to design a new Government House when Cary Castle burned in 1899. Lieutenant-Governor James Dunsmuir had Maclure incorporate some of the architectural features into the design of Hatley Castle. (BCARS)

The remains of Government House shortly after the April 15, 1957 fire. Vice-regal operations were housed temporarily in the Empress Hotel. James Dunsmuir's porte cochere survived and is part of the present building. (G. Castle photo)

The Construction Phase

Martin Segger

For this commission, the largest and most prestigious undertaking of his career, Maclure assembled the best of his contractors, tradesmen and craftsmen. The septuagenarian Thomas Catterall, who had built Craigdarroch for James' father and Burleith for James and Laura, returned to build Hatley Park as a general contractor. Dixon and Howes, as contractors for the carpentry and millwork, employed twenty-five skilled carpenters and joiners for the interior finishing. Maclure's friend, architectural sculptor George Gibson, created the vine and foliated

Former Royal Colwood Golf and Country Club clubhouse. After the fire of February 18, 1929, P. Leonard James and Hubert Savage designed an Elizabethan-style building. During the Second World War, the structure was used as a hospital. Latterly, Mother Cecelia Mary Dodd and several sisters used the former clubhouse as part of St. Mary's Priory extended care hospital. The building was demolished in 1987. (Barry F. King drawing)

The old Colwood Hotel housed some of the stonemasons working on the construction of Hatley Castle in 1908. It was originally owned by Andrew Bechtel, a former runner for President Lincoln. The building was demolished in March, 1936, and replaced by the present structure. (Barry F. King drawing)

wood and plaster detailing at his Shawnigan Lake studio. Local granites were quarried for building the walls, while Haddington Island andesite sandstone [used in the construction of the Parliament buildings 1893–1897] was brought in for the detailing of the sills, mullions and copings. Specialty materials such as the rose-coloured Arizona sandstone for the hall fireplace had to be imported. The stained glass was made in the art-glass studios of the London firm of Morris & Co. Exotic woods were brought in from the West Indies and Australia. The slate for the roof was from Westmoreland, England, where it was hand split.

[Local contractors such as Leslie Peatt hauled rocks lumber and other materials and were paid five dollars per day for driver, wagon and horses. Equipment and supplies were brought ashore after being barged over to the lagoon. A cable was laid across Esquimalt Harbour to supply electricity to Hatley Castle, and water was piped in, crossing what later became the golf links. James Dunsmuir and Joseph Sayward financed the

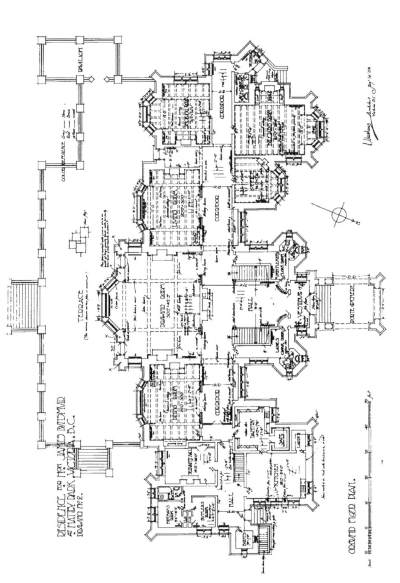

Ground Floor Plan of residence for Hon. James Dunsmuir at Hatley Park, dated January 1, 1908 and signed by Samuel Maclure, architect. The ladies' cloakroom is now the gentlemen's cloakroom and vice versa. The living room is now a bar room.

71

construction of the Colwood Golf and Country Club which attained "Royal" status officially in 1936. Others in the area were able to enjoy the convenience of power and water. Some of William Heatherbelle's sixty stonemasons were accommodated at the old Colwood Hotel.]

Entry would be through a massive carved oak door to an oak-lined vestibule with ladies' and gentlemen's cloak rooms on either side. The Tudor hall — revived by the English mid-nineteenth-century architects — was associated with romantic notions of the convivial, even democratic, life of the hall: the lord in his manor receiving, eating, drinking and making merry with his family, guests, and faithful retainers before an open fire. The decor called for Maclure's distinctive arts-and-crafts interpretation of Elizabethan revival, the play of subdued light from mullioned casements on half-timbered or wood-panelled walls, with a heavy light fixture suspended from the beamed ceiling.

A double staircase flanking the space was designed to rise along each wall, meet on a landing above the entrance and continue up to the gallery of the second floor. Many other features are of interest. A large hooded stone fireplace facing the visitor; tracery carved into blond oak detailing which is Gothic; Tudor arches with trefoil detailing; sliding doors on either side of the fireplace admitting entry to the drawing room; a corridor running the length of the house, intersecting the hall; and to the left (east) a corridor giving access to the dining room and kitchen wing. The dining room called for finishing in Douglas fir in an arts-and-crafts de-cor, with a beamed ceiling, panelled walls, large built-in glazed cabinets and tiled fireplace, and furnished with a large Jacobean dining suite on Axminster carpet. The large drawing room, treated in the traditional Maclure-Georgian manner, with coffered plasterwork, swag frieze and Grecian urn relief, is impressive. Crystal chandeliers and Ionic pillared fireplaces at each end of the 30- by 42-foot room, massive bay window and flanking arched French doors opening seaward on the terrace were important features. The colour scheme chosen was ivory and the fur-nishings green Louis Quinze. Turning to the living room, this was to be beamed and panelled in mahogany, and the smoking room to have yacca wood panelling framing leaded-glass bookshelves. On the north side of the corridor, panelling to plate-shelf height in oak wainscot in seventeenth-century style English oak was specified. A clubby atmosphere to the billiard room with large fireplace and inglenook was important, as was the study panelled in yellow cedar.

Large banks of casement windows, some detailed in fruit motifs and set in heavy sandstone mullions, were designed to catch vistas through formal gardens or out across the lagoon and to the Olympic mountains.

[The project called for 248 plans. A ground floor plan dated January 1, 1908, shows structural details and dimensions of rooms. The overall size, not including the porte cochere, is 86 by 200 feet. Steel beams over the main rooms are supported on stanchions to carry the upper floors of the multi-storey structure. Outer stone walls were lined with brickwork, and the interior west wall of the billiard room called for selected Clayburn bricks to a height of seven-and-one-half feet. Rubber tiles are shown for the washroom floors and nine fireplaces, including one in the servants' hall, size 14 by 20 feet and located in the east wing. Another drawing, the west elevation, indicates dressed stone for the chimneys, rough granite arches for doors and windows at the basement level, and local slate for the roof with its exposed rafters. The carved bargeboards in the gables were completed with varying patterns and two-by-eight-inch cedar was used for the half timbering and plaster between. Corbels on the tower were cut from stone to size nine by twelve inches. However, the terrace was not built according to the plan.]

The second floor contains five main bedrooms and three spare rooms, and in the left end wing there is a nurse's room, sewing room, and linen chamber. The hall and corridor are detailed but perhaps less lavish than below; the master bedroom, adjacent to the central hall, is Adamesque, with flanking boudoir and dressing room. The third floor is reached by newel stairs, off the staircase landing, and is devoted to guest rooms and dressing rooms. The fourth floor of the central tower contains a large ballroom [with a double-sided fireplace in the centre of the room].

These interior arrangements can be visualized from the outside, with the distinctive Maclure curve-mullioned windows defining the main interior spaces. On the south side, a two-storey crenellated granite range rises from the garden terrace and is dominated by a huge six-storey

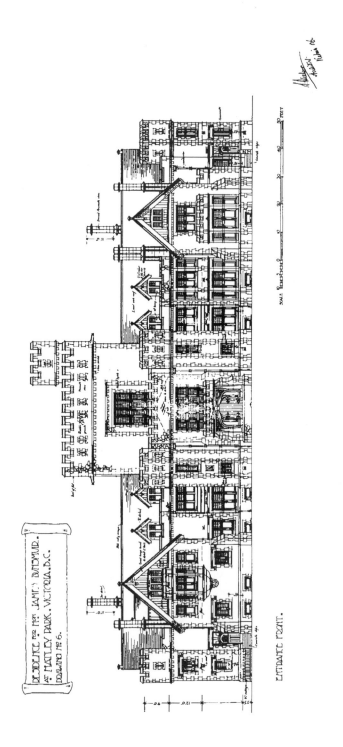

Front elevation of Hatley Park. Chimneys called for dressed Newcastle stone. Windows in the tower have leaded lights. Roof was to be of local slate.

castellated block, and a large bay window extends upward through three storeys. Within this squats the long saddle roof, broken by small gable dormers and anchored at each end by larger half-timbered gables whose huge cedar bargeboards are fretted into quatrefoiled tracery.

At the westerly end, a castellated bay marks the end of the axial corridors. A projecting gable wing contains the billiard room, and a generously proportioned block with battlements like the main tower contains the hall with attached octagonal towers that contain circular servants' stairs. On the east side of the wide Tudor-arched porte-cochere is a large gabled wing containing the kitchens and servants' rooms. Throughout, the main floors are of polished oak with inlaid gumwood.

Despite ultimate success in completion of the project [substantially completed within eighteen months], it is generally acknowledged that Hatley Park is not Maclure's best work. It looks back to the work of the English architect, Richard Norman Shaw, and the English arts-and-crafts. The magnitude of the undertaking came close to defeating the architect. Dunsmuir, a sombre and morose man, by this time was difficult to talk to. Much of the detailed decision making fell to Maclure in sole consultation with Laura Dunsmuir. [The biggest problem was to reconcile James' and Laura's entirely different perceptions of their home. Laura was happiest when she was entertaining and leading a very active social life. James, on the other hand, was the quiet, thoughtful, pipe-smoking man who enjoyed nothing better than hunting, fishing, his family and some male companionship.]

Hatley Park was vastly different in scale from Maclure's normal work, on which he lavished so much attention to design and construction details. Increasingly, design decisions and inspection work fell to Maclure's able head draughtsman, Douglas James. Maclure's organizational abilities, energy, and his health were taxed to the breaking point. Recognition of this by Mrs. Dunsmuir may well have provided the impetus for Maclure's trip to Europe on her behalf. To complete the work, Maclure made the trip to select and purchase furnishings at the request of Mrs. Dunsmuir. [Maclure took his wife with him, and they visited England and France, leaving Douglas James and his architect brother, Percy Leonard James, in charge of the work at Hatley Park.

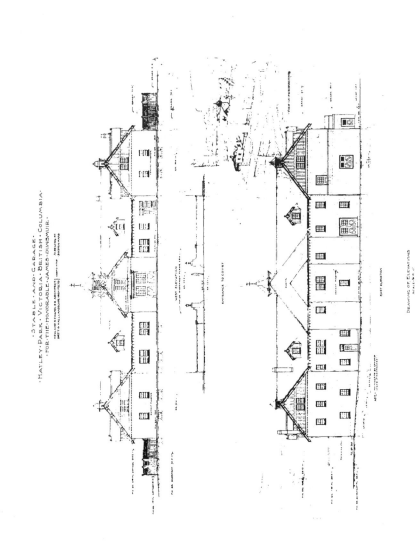

Elevation of stable and garage at Hatley Park. The architect was Howland S. Chandler, who was associated with Brett and Hall, the landscape architects commissioned by James Dunsmuir.

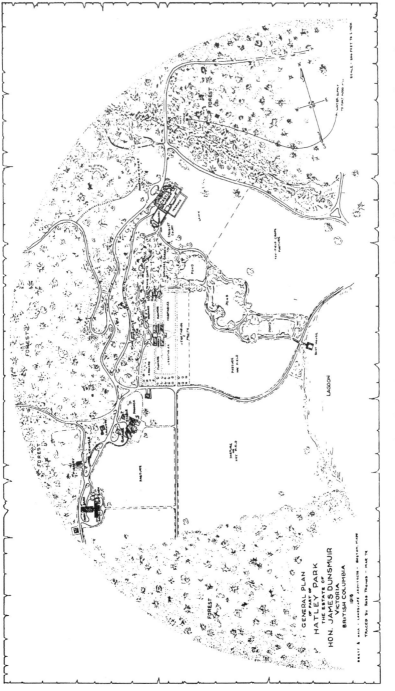

Plan of Hatley Park estate, produced by Brett and Hall, dated 1916. Shows main and outbuildings, forested and cleared areas, driveways, ponds and cultivated areas.

They were away for six weeks.]

Between 1913 and 1916, the landscape planning and development proceeded under the general direction of an outside consultant, Brett and Hall of Boston. Dunsmuir would have been familiar with the work of George D. Hall and Franklin Brett through their previous work in British Columbia, in particular the spectacular garden-city plans the firm had developed for the Grand Pacific Railway townsites at Prince Rupert, Prince George and Vanderhoof.

Among the features constructed under the Brett and Hall scheme were general visual improvements to the layout of the estate, the planting of formal gardens at the main house, and the development of a model farm. Grades were adjusted in the immediate vicinity of the house to improve the transition from buildings and gardens to the fringe of the surrounding spruce forest. The creation of a "Fountain Court" extending into the woods on the axis of the entrance porte-cochere was intended to produce a visual focus for the northerly elevation of the house. Two paths from this court through the "controlled" naturalism of the wood-land scenery led to the picturesque "Falls" and passed through groves of enormous hemlocks. A balustraded terrace adjacent to the westerly face overlooked an English croquet court. The terrace itself contained a formal Italian garden, dominated at the far end by a classical-style pavilion, itself flanked by circular loggias or pergolas, and terminated at each end by a vine-covered gazebo. This garden has intersecting gravel paths, each terminating at a statue of a Greco-Roman woman representing one of the four seasons.

Beyond the croquet court, farther into the woods, were built tennis courts and a secluded rose garden. Farther south, and commanding the vista over extensive pasture and hayfields stretching down to the lagoon, a large greenhouse was constructed, and around it in symmetrical layout an orchard was planted and cut-flower gardens, vegetable and fruit gardens were formed. Greenhouses led into the large conservatory which was prefabricated by the Ontario firm of Lord and Burnham. The conservatory became renowned for Dunsmuir's collection of rare Indian orchids, and a huge banana tree grew under the central dome. The old reservoir and drain dividing this area of the estate from the main house was reconstructed to form a pool in the centre of the walled rose garden, then drained off to form several brooks or rills which meandered down to the lagoon through three large ponds and connecting waterfalls, the main features of a Japanese garden. This garden was designed and planted by landscape architect and gardener Isaburo Kishita, whom the Dunsmuirs brought out from Japan to carry out the task for them. Later, he would construct Japanese-style gardens for other Maclure clients such as Mrs. Butchart and F. Barnard, Lieutenant-Governor of British Columbia from 1914 to 1919.

Different levels of the garden and its pools were interconnected with fish ladders so that the trout and salmon could swim unhindered through the entire course. The banks of the ponds were planted with native flowering trees, shrubs and herbaceous plants which formed a transition from these "contrived" areas to the fringes of the natural wooded parkland beyond. With a similar intent, the paddocks and pastures were enclosed by metal fences designed not to intrude on the landscape while containing the browsing cattle.

In 1913, an extensive granite wall was built along Sooke Road. Part way along, a stone lodge and handsome wrought iron gates were constructed.

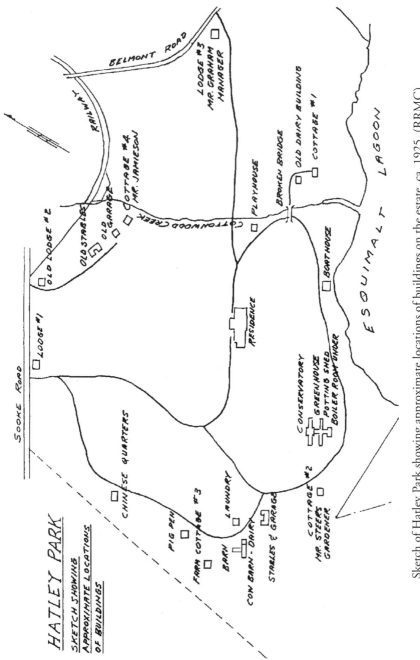

Sketch of Hatley Park showing approximate locations of buildings on the estate, ca. 1925. (RRMC)

Westerly wing of Hatley Castle under construction in the summer of 1908. (RRMC)

Photo taken from the porch of the Conway cottage. Easterly and northerly facades of Hatley Castle during construction in 1908. Contractor William Heatherbelle employed sixty stonemasons on the project. (William Conway Collection: EA V987.20.9 N150)

Hoisting a stone block in the construction of the easterly wing of Hatley Castle, July, 1908. (RRMC)

Architectural features abound. This oriel window on the north facade of Hatley Castle has mullioned windows and crenellated walling above. (G. Castle photo)

A recessed tablet on the front facade of the castle confirms the date of construction. Intertwined, in order, are the digits 1, 9, 0, 8. (G. Castle photo)

Specially designed ornamented cast iron downpipes re-affirm the date of construction, A.D. 1908. (G. Castle photo)

The door to the castle. The faces on each side represent James and Laura Dunsmuir. Above the doorway (centre) are the initials L, J, D. The tudor arch echoes the oak arches inside in the great hall. (G. Castle photo)

The great hall has two ascending staircases which lead to a landing part way up and then to a minstrels' gallery on the second floor. The elk head is from Dunsmuir's time and is a reminder of happy hunting times at Cowichan Lake, where he had a lodge. There is golden oak panelling, which is carried throughout the halls. The light fixtures, mostly pewter, are original. Fireplace is of Arizona sandstone. (PABC 63294)

The stained glass windows above the landing in the great hall were, according to legend, sent from England in barrels of molasses. However, Thomas Catterall suggested that wood shavings were more likely. The windows have art nouveau patterns of orbes and circles suspended by blue tendrils. (G. Castle photo)

There are a number of features in the dining room, which is panelled in quartered (Canadian) oak. This is a most expensive way to cut wood, but it enhances the grain. There are ebony and ivory inlays on the panelling. The built-in sideboard opened for serving. There are inlays of Australian beanwood in the flooring, and originally the carpet and curtains were blue. (PABC 63869)

The drawing room at Hatley Castle is in the Georgian style. Features to note are the "egg and dart" design, garlands and urns. The room was furnished with a deep green carpet, green silk-covered chesterfields, and chairs with cushions in pink and gold. The Steinway piano is now at Craigdarroch Castle. The master bedroom on the floor above was the same size (30 feet by 42 feet 3 inches). (PABC D-3026)

Statues in the garden add another dimension to the beauty and tranquility — timelessness. (G. Castle photo)

Conservatory at Hatley Park was supplied by Lord and Burnham of Philadelphia, and the glass came from France. It was designed ca. 1914, with the conservatory at Kew Gardens, Hampton Court Palace in England, in mind, for a reputed cost of $75,000. There used to be a banana tree growing under the dome. It was a full-time job for William Steers, the gardener. Sixty tons of coal and two hundred cords of wood a year were needed to heat the conservatory. (PABC 79967)

The garden stairway, constructed ca. 1913, led to a woodland area and was part of the landscaping project by Brett and Hall. Its main purpose was to be a visual delight from the main entrance to the castle. (PABC 79960)

An article from the *Florists' Review*, October 26, 1916, illustrates the conservatory and greenhouse. The conservatory had 58-foot wings 25 feet wide, and the palm house was 42 feet long. The greenhouse was 140 feet 8 inches long and 25 feet wide. Dunsmuir was never honoured with a title. The glass buildings were at Colwood, not Vancouver! (CCA)

The dairy and cow barn complex of the working farm at Hatley Park was built of brick and concrete. All milking was done by hand, but there were overhead feeders. Rubber bumpers protected the flanks of the cattle. View from the west. (CCA)

View of the Japanese garden and castle in the background from the lower lakes area. (PABC G-373)

View from the Japanese gardens. James Dunsmuir brought Isaburo Kishita from Japan to landscape this part of the grounds at Hatley Park. Among Mr. Kishita's other clients were Jenny Butchart and Sir Frank Barnard. (RRMC)

Southwest corner of the castle with some of the landscaping done. (PABC D-3020)

The south facade of Hatley Castle, with metal fence in the foreground marking the boundary between the lawn and fields or pastures. (RRMC)

Early picture of the easterly and southerly facades of Hatley Castle. The ivy has not yet grown, and the landscaping has not been completed. (PABC A-5528)

Ornamental waterwheel on the stream in a secluded part of the grounds, fed by a spring. (PABC E-2120)

Rustic gateway to one of the four ponds between the present-day library building and the lagoon. (RRMC)

View from the lower part of the lawn after landscaping completed in 1916. (PABC A-7782)

Sooke Road gatehouse (shown on the plan as Lodge No. 1). The gate system is a different design from the main gate at Belmont Road (Lodge No. 3). (PABC E-2127)

An Interview with Douglas James

Ginnie Beardsley

"When I went back to Hatley Park after many years, I thought, 'I must have had a double life — surely I can't be as old as that castle!'" says Douglas James, the architect who, under the supervision of his employer, Samuel Maclure, did the 248 working drawings from which the famous Dunsmuir residence was built.

As a matter of fact, Mr. James was but twenty years older than the stately home — strictly speaking not a castle at all — whose centuries-old appearance he helped to create.

Coming to Victoria in 1907 after serving his articles in London and being employed by the vice-president of the Royal Institute of British Architects, young Mr. James was able to answer "Yes" when Victoria's favourite society architect asked him, "Are you an English draughtsman?"

Much of Hatley's interior arrangements and the measurements of many of the rooms were derived directly from the Government House of the day of which the Honourable James Dunsmuir was then the occupant. The magnificent simplicity of the design is patterned after Compton Wynyates, the Tudor residence of the Countess of Warwick. Douglas James, as part of his training, had spent three weeks of each year sketching and measuring England's old and famous buildings, Compton Wynyates among them. His knowledge of its solid construction was of immense value at Hatley, the walls of whose centre tower are three feet six inches thick.

Mr. Maclure (who very rarely, if ever, met the quiet financial genius who employed him) let the contract to Thomas Catterall, the contractor of Craigdarroch and of much of the other Dunsmuir work. With his son, Harry, as superintendent, and his daughter as bookkeeper, the construction was going very well by August, 1908, so that while the architect was in Europe selecting furnishings, Douglas James was left entirely in charge of the project. "Quite a big load for a young fellow of twenty to carry in addition to all the other work they had going on."

Supervisory visits, which had to be made twice a week, each took a full day. Occasionally Mr. James would ride out by horse and buggy with Thomas Catterall. But more often he rode to the end of the Esquimalt carline with the workmen and boarded an ex-navy shore-leave boat, called the *Gentle Annie*, which was towed across Esquimalt Harbour by a big launch under the control of Sammy Doncaster. It was a cold and choppy ride in winter, and in any season the walk from Belmont Wharf to the work site was a long one.

The thick slates, in their soft green, which roof the main residence, the Sooke and Colwood gate lodges, the stables and the coach house, came by sailing ship from England. Mr. James recalled that:

"William Morris designed and made the beautiful stained glass leaded windows, and another Englishman, the architect Adams, designed the fireplaces; though their tiles are of American manufacture."

Exotic woods were generously used in the panelling of Hatley. Yacca — a very big-grained wood which comes from the West Indies — was used in Mr. Dunsmuir's study (the Commandant's office in the later times of Royal Roads Military College use) at the corner overlooking the Italian garden. Australian jarrah wood and rosewood were also used lavishly but tastefully. Mr. James recalled especially the pantry fittings being of rosewood. Panels were "framed" (built like a door) instead of being simply made of sheets of wood laid on the wall and battens fastened over the joints.

All work was done on a day-labour basis, with Mr. James checking the accounts and going to the castle to call for his employer's cheque. The remarkable feat of finishing this, the largest private residence of its time on the Pacific coast, in eighteen months, was not accomplished entirely without difficulties. Mr. James recalled an occasion when the work of one sub-contractor was delaying the whole project. "Mr. Catterall said, 'You'll have to get him in here and give him blazes.' The man in question was between 70 and 80 and I was a nervous young man, but we rehearsed it and carried it off and got things moving a bit faster," Mr. James recalled.

Gatehouse lodge on Sooke Road is built of granite and has a slate roof. This is where Charles Cladding lived with his family while he was employed on the landscaping of Hatley Park. (James Dodd drawing)

Water has played a major role in Hatley Park for as long as records have been kept. In the early days, all visiting British ships called at Rodd Hill for their water supplies, which came from springs on the south side of the property by a big wooden flume (which belonged to the War Office in London), right across in front of where the residence was later built. The discovery of a delightful glen with a waterfall and many dogwood trees was responsible for Mrs. Dunsmuir's initial interest in the property with its mile of waterfront.

The charming little granite gatehouse lodge on the Sooke Road, trimmed with Haddington Island stone to match the family residence and covered with Virginia creeper, was built with a kitchen fireplace (for which only clues remained after modernization).

The Belmont, or main gate lodge, a quaint mixture of granite, blue rock and half timbering, was never used for its nominal purpose. It became instead, in 1913, the residence of John Graham, Mr. Dunsmuir's agent (or manager) for the estate. Later, it was the headquarters of the

Colwood Detachment of the Royal Canadian Mounted Police.

[In 1977, the year of the first convocation and graduation of a fourth-year class at Royal Roads Military College, the institute seriously considered dismantling the Belmont gatehouse, numbering each stone and rebuilding it inside the property for use as a museum. At that time it was used as the Belmont Park Town Hall for the armed forces housing enclave, and as a meeting place for the Community Association. The Belmont gate pillars had been relocated some years before, when the stones were numbered and the gates reassembled at their present location].

An Early Newspaper Report of a Visit to Hatley Park

James K. Nesbitt

In the spring of 1910, a *Colonist* reporter visited Hatley Park and wrote:

"It is one of the most magnificent houses on the Pacific Coast. The terraces are miniatures of Blenheim Palace [the great Baroque mansion, seat of the Dukes of Marlborough at Woodstock, Oxfordshire, where Sir Winston Churchill was born in 1874]. The front of the residence spreads 205 feet and is of rubble granite laid in snail creep style with dressings of Saturna Island freestone.

"The stained glass windows have homey inscriptions such as 'Flora', 'Hebe', 'Pamona', 'Ceres' [the goddesses of the four seasons], and 'East, West, Home's Best'. The fireplace in the library is of green Rockwood

Stained glass windows in the former dining and drawing rooms have homey inscriptions. (G. Castle photo)

tiles surmounted by a heavy mantel inlaid with brass, ebony and mother-of-pearl.

"Mrs. Dunsmuir's bed-chamber on the second floor has wide bay windows overlooking the gardens and the sea to the mountains in Washington State. It features tones of white and pink. The walls are delicately tinted as the inside of a shell. The fireplace here is of pink tiles, and the mantel of white enamel with splashes of gold tracery."

[It was in this suite that Laura Dunsmuir died 27 years later in 1937.]

LIFE AT HATLEY CASTLE

Life at Hatley Castle

The Friends of Hatley Park Society
Historical Committee

Dunsmuir's release from public life came on Saturday, December 11, 1909, exactly two weeks before Christmas. On that day, Thomas Wilson Paterson was sworn into office as the new Lieutenant-Governor of British Columbia. He was wealthy, having made his fortune from contracting to build railways. He was the proud owner of a new Winton automobile which cost a fabulous $6,000.

Workmen were still doing the finishing touches at Hatley when James, Laura, and children "Boy", Emily, Joan, Jessie, Kathleen and six-year-old Dola moved in. Robin had married Maude Schoobert in November, 1901 and had built Allingham on the Esquimalt waterfront. This lovely Maclure-designed shingle-style mansion was completed in 1907 but was eventually demolished. Byrdie and Guy Audain were building a delightful chalet-style home, Ellora, on Foul Bay Road, designed by Maclure. (It is now the Wayside House Sanatorium). Elizabeth had married Henry Hope in 1907, and her sister, Laura had married Arthur Bromley in 1904. The Hopes spent some of the time in England and some of it in Vancouver, while the Bromleys had taken up residence in England.

Having satisfied his wife's desire to be chatelaine at Government House, Dunsmuir made arrangements early in 1910 to sell his mining interests for $11,000,000. He was beginning to appreciate Hatley Park life, and continued to enjoy his yacht. He was the first honourary commodore of the Royal Victoria Yacht Club, and the displacement of *Dolaura* helped the club to accumulate sufficient tonnage to pave the way to receive regal permission for the prefix "Royal" to be used.

Curiously, an article appeared in the *Colonist* in 1911 stating that: "James Dunsmuir, growing older at his magnificent Hatley Park, and frequently away at his fishing lodge on the Cowichan River, decided to sell his gleaming yacht *Dolaura*, in which he had entertained the Kaiser of Germany. The *Dolaura* is on the market at an approximate price of $125,000, which is half the amount she cost when Messrs. Fleming and Ferguson of Paisley, Scotland, built her in 1908. For some time she has been lying idle at Esquimalt."

Again in the *Colonist* (January 8, 1978), Katherine Wharf recalled the *Dolaura* days when her husband, George, was steward on the vessel. Dunsmuir also owned *Baroda*, a steel-hulled vessel which used to supply coal to the yacht and would tie up in Esquimalt Harbour opposite Todd's cannery. Katherine Wharf remembered that Muriel and Kathleen Dunsmuir attended Dr. Pope's private school at Hillside and Rock Bay. George Wharf, born in Surrey, England, had served in the Royal Navy, as did Captain Shenton, master of *Dolaura* and good friend of Dunsmuir.

Boy, to quote an old expression, was "the apple of his father's eye." Robin had spent huge amounts of money and was an alcoholic, to his father's dismay. So Boy would be the one to receive the bulk of the Dunsmuir wealth in due course. He attended Bolton's, named for one of the founders of the school, William Washington Bolton. This institution is now St. Michaels University School.

Boy's passion was horses. He may not have had a great amount of ambition, but horses brought out the best in him. The stables were built and horses acquired, usually with no expense spared, from as far away as England. One of Boy's favourites was a show jumper called Kismet. It was sent to Montreal, where Boy won the Open Jumping competition. At the time he was working in the Bank of Montreal and found it hard to keep a horse when he earned so little.

At home, Jessie Muriel rode Dog Fox, while Joan Marion rode one of Boy's favourite horses, a black beauty called Nigger. Boy would join them and Dola would follow on her pony. Their mad gallops beyond the walls of the estate would produce comments from nearby residents. Dola's nanny, Miss Easom, would probably have had something to say too.

In November, 1911, James and Laura left Victoria for a long holiday. They visited Switzerland, Egypt and England, among other places, over the next several months. Undoubtedly, the change was of great benefit to James, with the unwanted burdens of life long forgotten. The

Dunsmuirs returned to Victoria in the late summer with James looking forward to his retirement years at Hatley.

James loved to play games with his youngest child, Dola, and her nephew, Jimmy Audain, who was actually a few months older than his aunt. He liked to hear their laughter and happy screams in the recesses of the great house.

Even outside of Dunsmuir's domain, 1911 was a good year. Anglicans dusted off the plans that J.C. Malcolm Keith had drawn for the new cathedral some years before and discussed the construction, which would be assisted by a large amount of money provided by Laura Dunsmuir. Work began on a new building for the Union Club and, with the value of building permits having risen from less than $400,000 in 1900 to well over $2 million, carpenters lost all sense of proportion and began asking $4.50 for their nine-hour day. There were 4,200 telephones in Victoria, including the Dunsmuirs'. It was the year that George Langford, son of Captain Langford, who was born in Victoria in 1851, made a return visit after sixty years. He was enjoying retirement in England and was impressed with the changes in British Columbia's capital city. He still believed he was the first white child born in Victoria, but it was later discovered that William Whitlock was born two years earlier. Airplanes were being used to show that there was a future in flight. One flew over Victoria and took off the top of a tree near the Willows Race Track. The *Colonist* reported that "Little shrieks of consternation were heard from several of the ladies in attendance." The Dunsmuirs' former company, the E & N Railway, reached Cowichan Lake as well as Alberni.

While the Dunsmuirs were away, H.R. Macmillan was named Chief Forester of British Columbia, and Premier McBride became the first native-born British Columbian to be knighted. Victoria's sealing fleet, once a major industry, was sold at auction. As autumn 1912 approached, it was announced that an observatory would be built on Gonzales Hill. The contracts for Ogden Point wharf and for the first buildings at the University of British Columbia were let. A new theatre at the corner of Blanshard and Broughton Streets, tentatively called "The McBride", was planned, later renamed the Royal Theatre.

James Dunsmuir Imports a Car and Chauffeur

The original stables and garages were built north of the house up the hill. Dunsmuir made news in 1906 when he paid out $12,000 for a powerful limousine imported from Italy. Records at the B.C. Archives and Records Service list only one Italian car registered in British Columbia in 1906 — a Fiat. He probably was the first British Columbian to import a chauffeur along with the car. At the time the motorists of Victoria comprised a somewhat exclusive group, as there were only about 150 in the whole province. One of the earliest gas-driven cars in Victoria was an Oldsmobile which Dr. E.C. Hart purchased in 1903. Captain J.W. Troup had a Cadillac car bearing license number 2. (Licence number 1 belonged to John Barnsley, who had an Orient Buckboard runabout in 1904). Some well-known families who indulged in early motoring were the Todds of cannery fame, B.T. Rogers, R.P. Butchart, F.M. Rattenbury, and F. Barnard, who had the misfortune to be stopped and fined five dollars for not sounding his horn when going round a corner. No doubt James Dunsmuir was in good hands with Maastricht, his chauffeur.

Laying Out the Grounds

Early in 1913 Dunsmuir commissioned Brett and Hall, landscape architects of Boston, Massachusetts, to produce a general plan for the Hatley Park estate. George D. Hall and Franklin Brett had already produced plans for the Grand Trunk Pacific Railway at Prince Rupert and elsewhere in British Columbia. Over the next couple of years they improved the estate visually, planted formal gardens at the castle and laid out the model farm. The grades of the drives were improved, and they designed the "Fountain Court". A dozen Lombardy poplars would serve as a windbreak from the sea and protect the flower and vegetable gardens as well as the conservatory. The new garage and stable was one and one-half storeys, built of concrete and brick. In the stable, the stalls were of oak complete with nameplates for the animals. The dormered roof provided living accommodation for a number of staff. The complex had two wings and incorporated a courtyard area inside the gateway. The groom and his family resided in the easterly wing, and the chauffeur's quarters were in the opposite wing. Gas pumps and space for four cars enabled vehicles to be serviced on site.

The dairy buildings included a cow barn which accommodated about ten cows. Milking was done by hand, and there were overhead feeders. Corners of the building had protectors so that the flanks of the cattle would not be bruised. A silo was built on the dairy site, and there were two others nearby. An ice house and barn were part of this complex.

Some of the early buildings on the Hatley Park site have long gone. The place where contractor Thomas Catterall stayed during the construction period, dog kennels, piggery, ice house, smoke house and the building for the Chinese workers have left virtually no trace of their former existence.

Even disregarding the enormous capital outlay in constructing the buildings, silos, and related farm structures, the operation never was profitable, and this fact would be of some concern to Laura Dunsmuir in the 'thirties. It really mattered little when James Dunsmuir was alive, however.

Sarah Bernhardt was in Victoria in 1913, and the new Union Club building was finished. The YWCA took over the old one on Douglas Street. The Royal Victoria Yacht Club moved to its new quarters on Ripon Road in the Uplands. With the growing number of American tourists, some people suggested that it was time that the "rule of the road" be changed from left-hand to right-hand, but this had to wait until January 1, 1922.

Life Continues at Hatley

James and Laura indulged in their favourite activities. For James it was hunting, fishing, cruising with *Dolaura*, planning the layout of the estate, being a good husband and father, enjoying his "stable" of automobiles, smoking his pipe, having only an occasional drink (he never touched a drop until he was 50), and visiting his club (the Union Club). Some of his fellow members included his architect, Samuel Maclure, Francis Rattenbury, F.S. Barnard, one of the original members and who would in December, 1914 become British Columbia's next Lieutenant-

Governor, D.R. Ker of Brackman-Ker milling, Sir Richard McBride, premier of British Columbia, and Rev. Wilmot Baugh-Allen, all of diverse backgrounds and interests, which was, and still is, a main strength of the Union Club.

Laura continued to revel in entertaining, planning and managing the day-to-day running of the household with the able assistance of William Packe, the butler, John Jamieson, the footman, two able cooks, Gong and Hoy (who would be with the Dunsmuirs for fifty years) and the support staff. Laura devoted much time to charity work, holding garden parties and organizing promotional activities to help raise funds for worthy causes. She was also a great supporter of the Alexandra Club, which was established in 1900 as a ladies' alternative to the exclusively male Union Club. They met in rented premises on the east side of Government Street, between Broughton and Fort Streets. The building belonged to G.A. Kirk, a Union Club member who was married to Elizabeth Georgina Harvey, granddaughter of Robert Dunsmuir. In May, 1911, a splendid new club building financed by Laura was opened on Courtney Street. It boasted a ballroom and was later known as the Windermere Building. Meanwhile, Laura informed the recently formed Colwood Women's Institute that she would be most pleased if members would approve a motion to found a church in Colwood. Members met with Rural Dean W. Baugh-Allen to discuss the matter, and Mrs. Edith Peatt and other members got busy raising funds. Meantime, Anglican services were held in the Presbyterian Church. Mr. Alfred Peatt donated land, and the building was constructed near the old Colwood Hall. Laura attended the dedication service on October 26, 1913, with Bishop John Charles Roper, Dean Baugh-Allen and Rev. H.B. Hadlow officiating. Mrs. James Dunsmuir attended St. John the Baptist Church, and she paid off the debt on the vicarage and gifted the churchyard gates. Nearby, in the Pioneer Cemetery, are buried some of the people who worked on Hatley Castle, such as members of the Peatt family.

There was some excitement in the Dunsmuir house, as James and Laura's daughter Marion (Joan Marion) was soon to be married to Percy Stevenson, a sportsman, ardent traveller and reader. He was previously married, so that, when the ceremony occurred in England, November

19, 1918, Marion gained an instant family in the form of two young boys.

Early in 1914, it was announced that Alfred Yarrow, the British shipbuilder, had purchased the B.C. Marine Railway Company in Esquimalt, which was founded by Fitzherbert Bullen in 1893. Yarrow's son, Norman, would manage the yard, assisted by E.W. Izard, who later supervised the installation of the bells at Christ Church Cathedral. It is interesting to note that Izard's son, Arthur, later was a professor at Royal Roads Military College.

First World War — "Boy" Lost at Sea

Architect Francis M. Rattenbury, who was supervising the completion of a major addition to the Parliament Buildings, had recently returned from England with some disturbing comments which Derek Pethick quoted in his book, *Summer of Promise:*

"One of the amazing things about the situation in England is the absolute unanimity amongst all classes that war with Germany is inevitable. It is no longer a question as to whether there is going to be war, but of when it will break out."

On June 30, 1914, the *Colonist,* in a single column at the right of the front page, announced that the Austrian heir Archduke Franz Ferdinand had been assassinated, ending an era and setting the stage for a new age. Just five weeks later, on August 4, Britain declared war on Germany, the consequences of which were unimaginable.

Boy was enjoying a summer holiday at Hatley when the war started. Being crazy about horses, he volunteered for the B.C. Horse, a mounted militia unit organized by former cavalry officers. He was sent to Winnipeg on an officer training course, and when he returned to Victoria it was as a lieutenant in the 2nd Canadian Mounted Regiment. They kept up training, expecting to be shipped overseas, without any sign of being moved — time hung heavily, especially for Boy. He put in a request to resign his commission to join the Royal Scots Greys, which was originally called the Royal North British Dragoons. (W.C. Grant, first settler in the Colony of Vancouver Island at Sooke, was an officer in the Dragoons.)

Lieutenant James Dunsmuir was proceeding to England to obtain a commission in a British regiment and get to the front in France as soon as possible. He booked passage on a British ship, *Lusitania*, and left New York on May 1, 1915. There were fifteen Victorians aboard among 1,600 passengers. The German Embassy in Washington warned that passengers travelling on ships flying British flags did so at their own risk. At 3:10 on the afternoon of May 7, a few miles off the Irish coast, Kapitanleutnant Walther Schweiger sank *Lusitania* with a single torpedo. The reason it sank in just 18 minutes was because it carried fifty tons of shells, six million rounds of ammunition, and 3,800 forty-pound packages of explosives wrapped up as parcels of furs or cheese. German submarine U20 dived and sailed away. She had already sunk three freighters within a week. In Germany, commemorative medals were struck. As fate would have it, the U-Boat captain died by drowning two weeks later. As *Lusitania* could easily exceed her designed speed of twenty-four-and-a-half knots, which was about twice as fast as a submarine, it was perhaps unfortunate that she was steaming slowly before she was hit. It did not matter that her name had been painted out. Major Guy Audain, stationed in England, was granted leave to go to Ireland to try to find his brother-in-law among the recovered corpses, but to no avail. Boy was one of eight Victorians and one of the 1,198 passengers who lost their lives.

At Hatley Castle, James and Laura were torn with grief. In Boy were all James Dunsmuir's hopes and dreams — the level-headed, sober, responsible heir to the family fortune. James went into depression and played one particular record over and over — "Where, Oh Where Is My Wandering Boy Tonight?" Eventually he made some adjustment and reacted by donating funds to the war effort. He contributed hundreds of dollars each month for the duration to the Red Cross, and purchased half a million dollars worth of War Bonds. He was never the same person again. Laura had nightmares for the rest of her life.

With the passing of Boy, James Dunsmuir decided he would share part of the estate with his daughters. They received land in the estate, and he set up a trust fund on their behalf. Other than that, he did virtually no estate planning; consequently, like his father before him, he would leave his widow with the bulk of the estate and the responsibility of having to manage things.

In February, 1916, Hatley was under snow like the rest of Victoria. It was a record fall — as much as a metre in depth, with drifts much deeper. The army was called out to shovel the streets downtown. Algernon Pease, who supplied berry wine to the Union Club from his farm on the site of the present-day University of Victoria, had to hitch a horse to the sled and tow it down to the water at Cadboro Bay, where he loaded the cargo on to his speedboat, *Legal Limit*, and took it to Victoria's inner harbour for unloading and carrying the short distance to his customer on Gordon Street. At Hatley, John Graham, the estate manager, and Frank Hayward, head gardener, were concerned about the snow breaking the glass in the greenhouses.

It appears that James' yacht, *Dolaura*, was made available to the British Admiralty, and her crew went on active service. George Wharf, the steward, joined the Royal Canadian Navy and served for four years and eight months, but in 1915 he married Katherine Davis. She was the daughter of Captain James A. Davis, who was employed by the Dunsmuirs when they were living at Burleith. Mrs. Wharf recalled the chain gangs (from Topaz Gaol) shuffling past the Wharf house on First Street (later called Rose Street) where the Victoria and Sidney Railway operated. Captain Davis was first officer on *Thistle* and other Dunsmuir vessels. Captain Walter Bissett, who commanded *Thistle* when it burned in the Queen Charlottes area in 1907, was a good friend of the vessel's owner, James Dunsmuir. For a time his son, Dr. G.W.C. Bissett, lived in the former Audain house on Foul Bay Road.

In June, 1919, George Wharf was asked to go back as steward on *Dolaura*, which Dunsmuir had sold to the President of the Armour Packing Company. Even though he was a bad sailor (James Dunsmuir had to return from his visit to the Kiel Canal by regular steamship ten years earlier), he would miss her.

Kathleen ("Kat") was in England during the war and worked long hours at a soldiers' canteen. She met Arthur Selden Humphreys, a Royal Army Service Corps major. They were married in October, 1915, and came to Victoria when the war was over to live at Westover, near Government House.

James Dunsmuir Dies at His Hunting Lodge

James seemed to retreat more often to his rustic place by the Cowichan River. Sometimes he would spend weeks there with a daughter or a friend. On Saturday evening, June 5, 1920, he went to bed feeling ill, and died peacefully the next morning around 7 o'clock. His daughter, Marion Stevenson, and Dr. Hasell had gone to Cowichan Lake with him, while Laura and Muriel met Dola, who was returning from school in San Francisco. (She also attended St. Margaret's School in Victoria for a while).

James Dunsmuir left an estate valued at $3,597,583, with liabilities estimated at $265,066. During his lifetime he had donated hundreds of thousands of dollars to charity. He generously supported hospital treatment of consumptives. Perhaps significantly, Laura's mother died with tuberculosis. Now Laura had to continue as mistress of Hatley Park.

When James ("Jimmy") Audain heard about the death of his grandfather, James Dunsmuir, it was the end of term at Wellington College, a first-class private school near Reading, Berkshire. He returned home to Ellora in July and visited his bereaved grandmother at Hatley Castle. His eleven-year old sister, Laura, was still dressed in mourning. Mrs. Dunsmuir was still grieving very deeply, as were the aunts who had descended on Hatley upon the sad news of their father's passing. Jimmy's aunt, Dola, who had returned from California where she and her friend, Ruth McBride, daughter of a former premier of British Columbia, had been at school, entertained her nephew.

Jimmy easily recalled the wonderful memories of him and his aunt playing together. Good times went back to Burleith, where the Audains lived for a while when James Dunsmuir became Lieutenant-Governor and was at Government House. They played with Ronald Winter, the coachman's son. He would always remember when his grandfather gave him four one-hundred-dollar bills on his fourth birthday. Then, at Cary Castle (Government House), where Jimmy was installed while his parents were away, Dola's nurse, Miss Easom, ran the nursery like a barracks. When Jimmy locked himself in the bathroom and was unable to get out, the footman, John Jamieson, had to use a ladder to get inside.

Ellora was named after a place in India where Guy Audain, husband of "Byrdie", and son-in-law of James Dunsmuir, served with the British Army. The rustic chalet-style residence, sited on several acres on Foul Bay Road in Victoria, was designed by Samuel Maclure, and the Audains raised their children, James and Laura, here. Ellora eventually became a sanatorium for Christian Scientists. (Barry F. King drawing)

Probably the happiest times of all were when the children played their nightly games of "Bears and Indians" with James Dunsmuir.

On the other hand, Dunsmuir was a most punctual person. Meals had to be served exactly on time. He would even stand at the door to the dining room with watch in hand, as if he were doing a time and motion study. He could be as frugal as he could be generous. Once he had the car stop so that he could get a newspaper from the paper boy. When Laura asked what he was waiting for, he explained that there was a nickel change to come.

Jimmy enjoyed tea with Dola and Ruth at the doll (play) house by the glen on the Hatley estate, and this little cabin was undoubtedly the inspiration for Laura Audain's doll house under the big maple tree at Ellora.

The Dunsmuir daughters were left comfortably well off financially with the passing of their father, and with this newly found security they eventually left Hatley and their mother in the good hands of her faithful staff and the Scottish-born ex-rugby-champion estate manager, John Graham.

In 1921, Jessie Muriel ("Moulie") married Captain Edward Molyneux in France. He was decorated for bravery during the war and opened a fashion house in Paris. Moulie helped finance this very talented designer, and soon he was employing more than two hundred people in Paris and in Monte Carlo. Although it was a dazzling world for Moulie, the marriage was short-lived. However, she was married again in 1928 to Maurice "Tolly" Wingfield, who was at least a good story teller. The marriage was put asunder by fate when Tolly expired from overdosing himself with alcohol. Meantime, the couple built a house which they called Journey's End. It overlooks Esquimalt Harbour and is now the administrative building for Fort Rodd National Historic Park.

These were unhappy times for Laura Dunsmuir. Her daughter, Sarah Byrd, died at Pau, a Pyrenean resort in southwest France about ninety kilometres from the Atlantic coast. Her two children, Jimmy and Laura Frances, were twenty-one and fifteen years old respectively. Laura Dunsmuir had been immensely fond of her eldest daughter because Byrdie seemed more like a younger sister. Now that fondness would be transferred to Jimmy and to Laura, who spent some of her time with her grandmother at Hatley and part of it with her father and various aunts in England. When Jimmy visited Victoria in the summer of 1929, he was met by his sister and aunt Kat and they went to Westover, the house Mrs. Dunsmuir owned.

Hatley Park had changed since his visit in 1920. A financial crisis was developing in the United States. Staying with Laura Dunsmuir was Moulie, now divorced from Edward Molyneux. Marion Stevenson was there, as she was now a widow. Elinor, who would never marry, had forsaken the European casinos and was about to build a house in Comox (demolished by a developer in 1994).

Most of the partying at that time took place at Westover, for Laura Dunsmuir did not approve of the really wild parties at some of the gatherings. Entertainment at Hatley was not lavish, but there was a party with Sarah Byrd's friends and families invited to re-acquaint themselves with Jimmy. Laura Dunsmuir was in a virtually unique position as one of British Columbia's foremost women. As mistress of Hatley Castle and widow of James Dunsmuir, her word carried great weight, not only amongst her family, but in the social sphere. As a result, there were plenty of friends for the Audain children. Laura Dunsmuir thoughtfully placed the "Old Stables", a cottage on the estate, at their disposal so that they could live and party as they wished. Unfortunately, the parties were sometimes too much for Mamie, their housekeeper, and her reports to grandmother were not appreciated. Mamie relinquished her duties, but the parties, if anything, became more lively, and the drinks stronger, in those days of Prohibition. Friends from Washington would come and stay at Hatley, and 1931 was a lively year socially, with no thought of the economic depression and the hard times. Laura Audain, who learned to play golf in Pau, enjoyed playing at Colwood, the course her grandfather planned with his family and friends in mind. A frequent visitor of the young people at Hatley was Jack Matson, whose father was owner of *The Daily Colonist*.

Laura Dunsmuir, now in her seventies, continued to entertain her children and their families, and in late summer they would all go to the place at Cowichan Lake. But in winter there were not many visitors at Hatley. It was sometimes hard to make up a foursome for a game of cards. Often there would be Elinor, granddaughter Laura, and perhaps a friend from the city such as the family physician, Dr. Wasson.

Laura Dunsmuir had her ways of not being bored or lonely. She would call in a representative from one of the stores such as Weiler's and discuss new furnishings for the house, or she would have Packe drive her around the estate, which was a distance of at least six miles. Once a week, on Thursday, she would go into the city. James K. Nesbitt once had a paper route, when the *Victoria Times* was owned by Will Spencer of Spencer's Department Store (later, Eaton's), and recalled being at the Fort Street entrance of the Times Building when:

"Mrs. James Dunsmuir arrived from Hatley Park in her long, black, gleaming Packard, chauffeur-driven and sometimes with Packe the butler acting as footman, and opening the car door for Mrs. James.

What an equipage it was!

"The Dunsmuir estate had an office on the third floor of the Times Building, and it was presided over by Maurice Hills, an English barrister and solicitor of the old school. He was Mrs. Dunsmuir's advisor on matters legal and financial. I'm sure that more than once he told her she was spending too much and would have to cut down, otherwise Hatley Park might have to be sold at auction. Hills, in wing-collar and patent leather pumps, always descended from the third floor to meet the limousine, and escort Mrs. Dunsmuir by elevator, operated by a dearly loved Scotsman, Dave Porter, who, I think, had a wooden leg in place of a leg he lost in the war.

"I recall her (Mrs. Dunsmuir) as a grandmotherly sort of lady, snow-white hair, usually dressed in black with a band of purple around her neck, and from the velvet was a pearl, or a diamond, or perhaps a ruby or emerald, or something like that.

"She was a pretty old lady with a nice, kind smile. Her day-a-week at the old Times was a very big day indeed, for often the chauffeur playfully tossed chocolate bars up and we all scrambled to catch them and fight over them."

Maurice Hills was a character. As a young barrister and solicitor, he went to San Francisco looking for a posting, certainly not a job. He saw a newspaper advertisement for a solicitor and went for an interview. Hills explained that he was a solicitor from England. "Good," said the man. "We expect 100 subscriptions a day. I hope you are a fast-talking solicitor." Disgusted, Hills headed for Victoria, where he found a "position" with the Dunsmuirs. Hills lived the rest of his life in Victoria, except for a disappointing visit made to London, where he found things too American. When he retired, he lived at the Union Club, where he always dressed for dinner even though he was the only one to do so.

Laura Dunsmuir's kindness is recalled by many people. Mrs. Mona Hansen, who still lives in Victoria, remembers that she and her sister stayed at Hatley several times with their former nurse, Jessie, who was employed in the Dunsmuir household as housekeeper after leaving Mona's family. Things were run very much like in the old country. She also recalls Packe, the butler, and that Mrs. Dunsmuir was very kind to the servants. She let Jessie show the girls all over the castle, but the place was always called Hatley Park, not Hatley Castle. Margaret E. Duck, formerly Margaret Plunkett, was Mrs. Dunsmuir's nurse for a time in the 'thirties and lived in at Hatley. She found Mrs. Dunsmuir to be a very fascinating lady who talked about the early history of British Columbia and her own life as chatelaine at Government House and Hatley Park, as well as the interesting guests she had entertained.

Irene Dalley's mother, uncle and aunt were living at the orphanage, and were picked up by Mrs. Dunsmuir from time to time and taken to Hatley, where they played in Dola's play house, always sure to please youngsters.

Laura Frances returned to England to be with her father, Guy Audain, while Jimmy stayed on at Hatley in the Old Stables with "Udder", a Chinese houseboy, to take care of things. By this time Jimmy had a real problem with his drinking, tried unsuccessfully to reform, and went back to England.

Movie Making at Hatley

Kathleen Humphreys always thought she should be an actress. Now that her marriage to Selden had fallen apart, she was ready to pursue a film career. So she left her California-Spanish-style house on Prospect Place in Oak Bay and headed for Hollywood. She probably realised that it would be most difficult to break into movies at forty years of age, so she entertained producers, hoping to provide investment money in return for acting parts.

In 1927, Britain took a major step to protect its motion picture industry by means of a quota system. It meant that twenty percent of the films distributed would have to be made by a British entity within the British Commonwealth. Kenneth J. Bishop heard about Kathleen. He was born in Britain and had dabbled in many aspects of the film industry for twenty years or more. In 1932 he formed Commonwealth Productions, which was registered in British Columbia. Bishop was president of the company, and Kathleen was a major financial backer. A building in the Willows Fairground in Oak Bay was made over into a studio, and, early in 1933, production commenced on *The Mystery of Harlow Manor*, utilizing some of the main features of Hatley Park and providing Kathleen with a small acting role. This was not completed. Instead, Kathleen invested more money in another film, *The Crimson Paradise*, in which she was the co-star. The film was shot at Hatley Park and at Cowichan River. Playing small parts were Laura Audain and Robin's daughter, Laura Marion, together with her brother and cousin. William Packe, the butler at Hatley, was also in the film, playing himself. Daphne Pooley, daughter of a former attorney-general, and Barbara Twigg, daughter of a former Deputy Speaker of the Legislature — friends of Kathleen — were also in the picture. Eighteen-year-old Mike Heppell was one of the actors and thought the film cost fifty to sixty thousand dollars. That was a fortune in the dark depression days.

The book on which the film was based was originally called *The Crimson West* and described a young man from Vancouver who sought the great outdoors in the Cariboo, where he met a local girl. The movie script changed the big city locale to Victoria and used the Dunsmuir residences, Hatley Castle and Craigdarroch Castle, as well as the Butchart Gardens (no charge to visitors in those days) and Beacon Hill Park, for locations. The film was completed in ten weeks.

Screening the film was a problem, since none of the Victoria movie theatres, especially those controlled by U.S. interests, wanted to take a chance on showing the first fully talking picture made in Canada. Arrangements were made for the showing after Ivan Ackery, manager of the Capitol Theatre, gained grudging approval from Famous Players. There was a catch, however. The film had to be shown in the last three days of the week before Christmas — quiet time — and after regular shows. The name of the film was changed to *The Crimson Paradise*, and it also had a modified script. A young, rich Bostonian is sent to British Columbia after graduating from university and a disagreement with his father. He joins a logging outfit and falls in love with the boss's daughter, who already has a boy friend. The two men try to get rid of each other, and the climax of the film is a fight in a cable car.

Ivan Ackery probably had no need to have 20,000 leaflets advertising the film dropped on Victoria from an aircraft. At 11:00 pm on Thursday,

117

December 14, 1933, with a sell-out audience, Ackery, dressed in tuxedo, welcomed Premier T.D. Patullo, Mayor David Leeming and other dignitaries, Dunsmuir family and friends, and patrons who cared more for familiar scenes than just to be able to criticize a poor movie, which, according to many, it was. Kenneth Bishop introduced the cast — live. The grand premiere proved to be a most enjoyable event, provided that the plot, acting and lines could be accepted or ignored. Next the film went to the Pantages Theatre in Vancouver, after which it went to England and appeared to vanish forever.

Bishop's Commonwealth Productions was in deep financial trouble. The other creditors had welshed, and subsequently Bishop managed to obtain more funds from Kathleen. Then, about a year later, she was informed that she was liable for the debts of Commonwealth's creditors. Her loans were unsecured, and she was unprotected. Bishop came out all right, formed another company, and made more films. Kathleen's capital funds, and her acting aspirations, were only a memory. She moved into an apartment in the Old Stables until she received some more money from her mother, Laura Dunsmuir. Kathleen then moved into Ellora, the Audain house on Foul Bay Road, where she could enjoy her natural lifestyle — entertaining.

More bad tidings came for Laura Dunsmuir when she received news of her youngest offspring, Dola, and of her divorce from Henry Cavendish ("Dish"). It did not even seem that six years had passed since their lavish wedding from Hatley Park in August, 1928. No one could forget the cortege, preceded by two police motorcycles with sirens sounding, followed by the deputy chief of the BC Provincial Police, Bob Owens, leading the wedding car all the way to Christ Church Cathedral. Following the service, the couple ducked under an arch of crossed swords. They made their home in London, where Dish indulged himself in horses and betting, having retired from the navy. Dola bought an interest in a dress shop.

Dola had a long friendship with Tallulah Bankhead which began in London in 1925. Both women were in their early twenties. Tallulah came from an Alabama democratic family and went on the New York stage when she was sixteen. Between 1923 and 1930 she was the scandalous idol of the theatre in London. Dola adored her all her life. Marion and Muriel enjoyed a dazzling life in conspicuous venues, spending money and gambling. They would come to Hatley and ask mother for more funds. Another summer visitor to Hatley was Laura (Maye), who had married Arthur Bromley back in 1904. Five hundred people attended the wedding reception at Burleith. As Lady Bromley, Maye became the only Dunsmuir to acquire a title. This was a good marriage.

The Sunset Years at Hatley

Laura Dunsmuir's health was deteriorating, but she remained interested in having visitors and in watching over the estate. William Steers, who did nothing else except look after the conservatory, recalled taking flowers up to the house and filling the rooms every day. After a time, Mrs. Dunsmuir regarded the conservatory as an extravagance. It was the most expensive feature in the estate, and quite a distance from the house. Once in while, a Dunsmuir daughter would drive over in her car and pick out a white orchid to wear to a dance.

Maurice Hills, the family solicitor, was concerned about the cost of maintaining Hatley Park in the bad economic times ($15,000 a year), and advised Laura Dunsmuir to establish a trust fund with the Royal Trust Company, with estate manager John Graham and two daughters as managers. She decided to leave the rest of her estate to her children or, if they were deceased, to their children.

Charles E. Sherwin, the chauffeur at the time, looked after the cars and trucks at Hatley and took Mrs. Dunsmuir for regular short drives. She had an elevator installed so that she would not have to climb the stairs. Visitors became fewer, but she could look back with satisfaction on the memories of visits from well-known people —Winston Churchill, the Duke of Windsor (when he was Prince of Wales), Lord and Lady Willingdon, Lord and Lady Byng, the Duke and Duchess of Connaught, Governors-General of Canada, Dame Nellie Melba — the famous Australian opera singer — and many others listed in the guest book which was donated to the B.C. Archives (now B.C. Archives and Records Service).

Laura Dunsmuir died on August 3, 1937. She was in her eightieth year. She had realised that there was no one in the family who could take charge of and maintain Hatley Park. None could afford to live there, and probably none really wanted to live there and carry the responsibilities. The daughters, by their very nature, were unlikely to get together and plan a strategy for the estate. Land subdivision and building starts were at their lowest ebb, so Hatley Park was simply a white elephant.

The trustees had instructions to sell Hatley Park. Laura Dunsmuir left $2,334,903. She did not forget her servants, nor Maude, the widow whose husband, Robin, died in 1929. There was no one around who could pay anywhere near the valued amount of Hatley ($260,000) and who could afford $1,500 a month or more to run the place!

The funeral procession left Hatley Park on Thursday, August 5, and Dean C.S. Quainton officiated at the Christ Church Cathedral service. Laura Dunsmuir was buried in the family burial plot at Ross Bay Cemetery, where there is a massive, polished grey granite pedestal with cornice and a pediment, topped by a draped urn. A grey granite curb surrounds the plot.

In the spring of 1938, Hatley Park was advertised for sale in England in the magazines *Mayfair* and *Country Life*. Douglas Flintoff, who founded the Victoria Amateur Movie Club in 1934, made a short film to attract buyers; it was sent to California. With little prospect of a sale in the near future, John Graham did what he could to help the estate reduce its running losses. He sold as much farm produce as possible, as well as commodities from the kitchen garden, orchard, greenhouse and conservatory (white orchids imported from India fetched $5 to $20 a pot).

On Wednesday, July 27, of that year, the estate was open to the public and was the scene of the Annual Garden Fete held by the Florence Nightingale Chapter, IODE, from 10:00 a.m. to 5:00 p.m. The invitation was extended to out-of-town visitors. In May, 1939, Graham opened the grounds for a charge, but the response was generally disappointing. That was the month King George VI and Queen Elizabeth visited Canada and saw Hatley Park while in Victoria.

On Thursday, June 1, 1939, at two o'clock in the afternoon, Maynard and Sons opened an unreserved five-day auction under instructions from John Graham. There were 927 lots, and among the items to be sold were the billiard table and grand piano. An out-of-town bidder, Sir Edward Beatty, bought the billiard table. It was enormously heavy and quite large to handle. Happily, this successful bidder decided to let the table stay in the billiard room as part of the house, the fate of which was as yet undetermined. Laura's magnificent Steinway grand piano, which the Dunsmuirs purchased for $4,000, was sold to Dr. T.A. Rickard for $500. When the doctor died, it was one of the Dunsmuir daughters who bought Hadleigh, the Rickard residence. She attended the auction for the furnishings and acquired the Steinway grand piano with her successful bid of $2,950. Many years later, the piano was purchased by Craigdarroch Castle Society for $55,000; it may be seen in the drawing room of the former residence of Joan, widow of Robert Dunsmuir.

Bidders had a field day, and now the former James Dunsmuir possessions are scattered far and wide. Recently, Dr. S.W. Jackman, who owned four handsome candlesticks from the Dunsmuir collection, donated them to Government House. One of the tasks of the Friends of Hatley Park Society is to make an inventory of the items sold in 1939 and to record their present location; they are an important part of the heritage of Hatley Park.

With war clouds approaching once again, the prospects of selling Hatley worsened. Garfield Weston's name was mentioned as a possible buyer, but the war had started at the beginning of September and still there was no purchaser.

By 1940, Hatley Park had to be sold. The federal government offered the trustees of the Dunsmuir estate $75,000, which worked out to be little more than one hundred dollars per acre with the castle thrown in. Hatley Park was no more. Henceforth it was to be known as Royal Roads, and the castle was to be used as an officer training establishment for sub-lieutenants. Or, it could be New Windsor Castle or Buckingham Palace West for the Royal Family, in the event of a German invasion of Great Britain.

The coaling hulk *Baroda* refueling *Dolaura* (named for Dola and Laura) in Esquimalt Harbour, November 24, 1910. There was a place east of Bombay in India called Baroda (now changed to Vadodara). (BCARS ZZ 95020)

His yacht provided happy times for James Dunsmuir, and it became well known on the east coast of Vancouver Island. (BCARS 27379)

Dolaura. This 218-foot vessel was built on the Clyde for a cost of $200,000 in 1908. (CCA)

In 1912, James Dunsmuir and Joseph Sayward had the foresight to purchase 240 acres of the old Hudson's Bay Company Esquimalt farm for $183,722, and the Colwood Golf and Country Club was born. The land was held by the Colwood Land Company; its shareholders were Biggestaff Wilson, Thomas W. Paterson, Frederick B. Pemberton, C.F. Todd, and Francis M. Rattenbury. The club house served as a hospital in the Second World War, and these temporary quarters later became the Chez Marcel restaurant on Island Highway. (Royal Colwood Golf & Country Club)

Westerly facade of the stable-garage complex. The Dunsmuirs had four cars and some trucks for use on the estate. Maastricht's quarters were over the cars. When Dirk F. Van Maastricht retired in 1928, Sherwin became chauffeur. (RRMC)

Old garage at Hatley Park which was located next to the old stables (now suites). Garage demolished. (RRMC)

View from upstairs window of the main gate house at Belmont Road at the time of the great snowfall, February, 1916. (RRMC)

The great snowfall in the winter of 1916 effectively stranded many homes in the outlying parts of Victoria. At Hatley Park, the best and only way to get around the estate was by horse and sleigh. (RRMC)

Haying in the area which later became the soccer field of Royal Roads Military College. (RRMC)

Gatekeeper Eng and his wife. (CCA)

Francis Phillip Hayward,
head gardener (right), and helper.
(CCA)

General view of the north side of Hatley Castle. Note the oriel window under the left gable, porte cochere, massive drop finials on the main gables, and crenellation. The heating plant was coal fired until 1977, when it was converted to oil. (RRMC)

The grand piano which used to be at Hatley Castle was sold at the auction in 1939 to Dr. T.A. Rickard. It is now in the drawing room at Craigdarroch Castle. (G. Castle photo)

Dola Cavendish's house, Dolaura, when it was almost ready for occupancy. Shutters have not yet been added to the windows, nor has the patio been built. (RRMC)

Dola Cavendish on the terrace of her home, Dolaura, set in twenty-three acres which were given to her by her father. Here she cared for her sister Kathleen's children when their mother was killed in a London air raid in 1941. It was also here that she entertained her friend, Tallulah Bankhead. (CCA)

A corner of a room in Dola's house with one of her prized possessions — a small grand piano made by Blüthner of Leipzig. Note also the picture of actress Tallulah Bankhead. (RRMC)

129

Same room, looking in the opposite direction. Note the oak multi-purpose table with spiraled gate legs and the picture of Dola's father, James Dunsmuir. (RRMC)

"Moulie" (centre) with Laura Mitchell (left) and Dola Wasson at the Metropole Hotel in Monte Carlo in the early 'fifties. (RRMC)

Sunroom, porch and part of garden at Journey's End, built in 1932 by Jessie Muriel ("Moulie") and Maurice ("Tolly") Wingfield, Moulie's second husband. (RRMC)

R.J. (Robin) Dunsmuir on a visit to Hatley Park. He lived in a waterfront home at Ten-Mile Point, designed by architect John di Castri. Robin was a grandson of James Dunsmuir. (Private Collection)

The bedroom of James and Laura Dunsmuir in 1942, when it was in use as the library for HMCS *Royal Roads*. (RRMC)

Gates at main entrance to Hatley Park before they were removed and rebuilt farther west. Each stone was numbered to facilitate the task. This was the residence of the estate manager, Mr. Graham. (RRMC)

Epilogue

Geoffrey Castle

Emily Elinor Dunsmuir died in April, 1938, only eight months after her mother. The six surviving Dunsmuir daughters, who were scattered about, took the news of the sale of Hatley for $75,000 with a certain amount of disappointment. Kathleen had left Ellora after the passing of her mother and moved to Switzerland. When the war started she went to England, where she did volunteer work at the Beaver Club Canteen for Canadian service personnel in London.

On March 8, 1941, Kathleen and her family and friends were celebrating the wedding of Kathleen's twenty-one-year-old son, Jim, to Joan Griffiths, at the Café de Paris, when a 250-pound high-explosive bomb made a direct hit on the building, killing eighty people. Kathleen Humphreys was among the dead, but the newlyweds escaped with injuries.

It is significant that two of James and Laura Dunsmuir's children died at the hands of the enemy in two world wars. On the other hand, fate decreed that one member of the family should not be put at risk, for James Audain, Kathleen's nephew, decided to leave the party just before the disaster happened. Fate also spared another young couple that Saturday night. Actor John Mills (later, Sir John) and playwright Mary Hayley Bell, married a few weeks earlier on January 16, had booked a table at the Café de Paris and were looking forward to enjoying Snake-hips Johnson and his band. However, as he was getting ready to go out, Mills suddenly decided he did not want to go to the cabaret, so his wife agreed that they should cancel. Instead they took their dog, Hamlet, for a walk in the park. The next day they heard about the destruction of the Café de Paris, and the consequent great loss of life, on the BBC news.

In her book *The Dunsmuir Saga*, Terry Reksten points out another remarkable parallel. "It was only after Kathleen's ashes were shipped home to Victoria to be interred in the family plot at Ross Bay Cemetery that someone remembered, with a chill creeping up his spine, that the

Café de Paris had been modelled on the Palm Room of the *Lusitania*."

Dola still owned part of Hatley Park. Some years back her father, who doted on her, gave her twenty acres of waterfront property below the Belmont gatehouse. When Kathleen was killed, Dola was staying with her actress friend, Tallulah Bankhead, who lived on an exclusive estate near New York. Dola thought she should take care of Kathleen's younger children and returned to her house, Dolaura, named for her father's yacht, and made preparations to raise her motherless nieces.

Dolaura, a late 'thirties English Arts and Crafts style one-and-a-half-storey house, was built of brick. Attractive features were dormers with half-hipped and sloping roofs, tall chimneys, and shuttered windows. French doors opened onto a patio. Gently sloping lawns extended to the water, and there was an unobstructed view of the sea and the Olympic mountains. Dola was always fond of dogs and flowers, and she also enjoyed Tallulah Bankhead's visits. Dola received a share of her sister

Dolaura (Cavendish House) was Dola's place. She hosted her close friend, Tallulah Bankhead, here. She was the last survivor of James and Laura Dunsmuir's children, and died in 1966. The house was owned for a time by Pam Ellis. It was also used as a Fort Rodd National Historic Park administration office until the office moved into Journey's End, Dola's sister Moulie's former home. (Barry F. King drawing)

St. John the Baptist Church, Glencairn Lane, Colwood, was built in 1912 and dedicated the following year. This Carpenter Gothic style structure was designed by H.O. Miles and constructed with funding from the Women's Institute and Mrs. Laura Dunsmuir. The land was donated by Alfred Peatt Sr. The interior has varnished natural wood, and there are open rafters in the ceiling. Dola Frances (Dunsmuir) Cavendish is buried in the churchyard. Church services are no longer performed, but the cemetery is still in use for cremated remains. (James Dodd drawing)

Marion's $335,248 estate when she died in Monte Carlo in May 1952. In 1959 Dola Cavendish advertised for some domestic help, and Arthur and Alice Holmes, recent arrivals from England, responded and were taken on. Alice was the housekeeper, and her husband acted as gardener and handyman. They lived in at Dolaura and were in Dola's employment for several years. Dola's health gradually worsened, and she died in 1966. She was buried at St. John the Baptist Church in Colwood. The last of James and Laura Dunsmuir's children was gone. She had belonged to the third generation of that family in British Columbia.

With each passing generation, memories of the Dunsmuir era become diluted and fragmented. People with first-hand knowledge are very few. Charles Cladding was employed on the landscaping at Hatley. His granddaughter, Alice, was at Hatley, and the gardener told her that the alyssum being planted near to the house would perpetuate her name. Alice, at age 90, recalled this clearly. Her uncle was Harry Catterall, who built Hatley Castle. Bill Cooper's father was the groundsman at Hatley, working for Mr. Eng, who lived in the Belmont gatehouse. (The Claddings lived in the Sooke Road gatehouse). Mr. Cooper remembers John Jamieson driving the truck around the estate. Francis Phillip Hayward was head gardener until Cecil Blogg took over. Later, Blogg's stepson, Bromley Davis (Dave) Quinney, did the job. Phil Simpson, whose father owned Producers Sand and Gravel Company, which had a right-of-way through the grounds of Hatley Park, recalls repairing the water pipe on the castle grounds in the 'thirties. He met John Jamieson, who had in his possession guns which had been left to his father by James Dunsmuir when he died. According to his grandson, Peter Bugslag was employed by the Dunsmuirs for more than fifty years. He was a bridge foreman on the construction of the E & N Railway and built one of the first houses and coal bunkers in Ladysmith. In later years he lived in the grey shingled house at the entrance to Royal Roads, and was a general handyman about the castle. A.P. Bugslag, the grandson, also recalled that, as a boy, he and his brother played in the Hatley Park woods and gathered armfuls of Lady's-slippers.

The largest ant hills he ever saw were there too. Peter Bugslag's son worked at Hatley before becoming a building contractor. He built Elinor

Dunsmuir's house at Comox Hill, "which later became a guest house for Crown Zellerbach people." It was he who renovated the stables for an apartment for Mrs. Selden Humphreys (Kathleen Dunsmuir).

These stories, related currently, are based on conversations with parents and grandparents, or personal memories of sixty to eighty years ago. Working for the Dunsmuirs was a way of life, and it was not perceived in an historical scenario. The story of an American military man standing in at the birth of James Dunsmuir at Fort Vancouver as godfather to the child (see Agnes Carne Tate, *Colonist*, September 11, 1966), needs further research to establish whether or not the soldier was the future U.S. president, General Ulysses S. Grant. We do not know why Robert Dunsmuir's name appeared on his marriage certificate as Dunsmore (Nesbitt, *Colonist*, September 11, 1977). Burleith, the Dunsmuir mansion in the Gorge area, perhaps really derived its name from Barleith, a place in Ayrshire.

What about Kathleen's film? It would have been acetate film — the kind used until the forties — which was very flammable and not particularly durable. Unfortunately, chances of a copy still existing are very slim, as more than sixty years have passed since the film was last seen in Vancouver and possibly in Britain. Fortunately, the real-estate film made as a sales promotion for Hatley Castle has been preserved and copies made.

The exterior of the castle remains virtually unchanged. Most of the interior changes are on the third floor. Quite early on, when the Canadian Government acquired Hatley Park, bedroom partitions were removed to make room for dormitories, and the stables were converted to classrooms. The conservatory, already abandoned because of the tremendous expense of maintaining it, was used for navigational instruction. A heavy snowfall in 1954 damaged the aging structure, so it was dismantled. All that remains is the stone foundation. Meantime, classrooms, workshops for welding instruction, and a drawing office were set up in the barn. The dairy was later converted to a physics laboratory.

More recently, film crews and actors have worked in and around the castle, stirring memories of Kathleen Humphreys and *The Crimson Paradise*.

The observant visitor will notice the original hot-water heating radiators in the rooms, the marks of the stone-cutting disks on the mullions, the year "1908" clearly cast on the exterior downpipes, the old tiling in the bathrooms, and the stags head above the fireplace in the great hall.

There can never be any doubt that the Dunsmuirs have taken their place in the annals of British Columbia history along with the Douglases, the Helmckens and the Pembertons. Their combined impact in those formative years is inestimable.

What of Hatley? Perhaps a quotation from "Another School", published in *Monday Magazine*, May 7–13, 1987, conveys one person's feeling yet represents many others:

". . . The sun has already fallen low in the sky, the last thick bars of sunlight shining through the branches of the fir trees as the temperature drops. On the edge of the deserted playing field, deer have gathered; four of them sit unmoving by the trees in oblong patches of sun. They do not stir . . . but sit together watching with wise brown eyes, their calmness and serenity seem to be a reassurance. 'LOOK,' they say, 'THERE IS NOTHING TO FEAR'."

When James Dodd, a Colwood artist, made this sketch of Hatley Castle in 1988, the walls were covered with ivy. The eighty-two-foot-high tower housed a ballroom on the fourth floor. The westerly facade overlooks the Italian Garden.

Like many of the ancilliary buildings, the dairy barn underwent changes. Within a year or so of the government having purchased the estate, this building was converted into classrooms and a workshop for the engineering department. It later housed the physics laboratory. View from the east. (G. Castle photo)

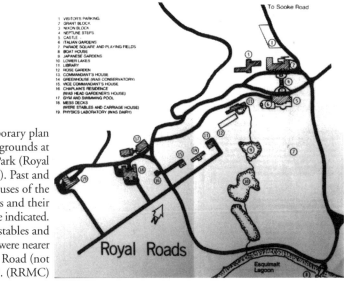

Contemporary plan of the grounds at Hatley Park (Royal Roads). Past and present uses of the buildings and their locations are indicated. The old stables and old garage were nearer to Sooke Road (not on plan). (RRMC)

1 VISITOR'S PARKING
2 GRANT BLOCK
3 NIXON BLOCK
4 NEPTUNE STEPS
5 CASTLE
6 ITALIAN GARDENS
7 PARADE SQUARE AND PLAYING FIELDS
8 BOAT HOUSE
9 JAPANESE GARDENS
10 LOWER LAKES
11 LIBRARY
12 ROSE GARDEN
13 COMMANDANT'S HOUSE
14 GREENHOUSE (WAS CONSERVATORY)
15 VICE COMMANDANT'S HOUSE
16 CHAPLAIN'S RESIDENCE
    (WAS HEAD GARDENER'S HOUSE)
17 GYM AND SWIMMING POOL
18 MESS DECKS
    (WERE STABLES AND CARRIAGE HOUSE)
19 PHYSICS LABORATORY (WAS DAIRY)

To Sooke Road

Royal Roads

Esquimalt Lagoon

139

The stables look much the same as they were in 1914. In 1941, the fine oak horse stalls were dismantled and the brass plates with the horses' names vanished. The space became classrooms. In 1964, the stable building was changed into a new facility with bar, games room and lounge. Then, in 1981, it was converted to a social centre for cadets and non-commissioned officers. (G. Castle photo)

The conservatory was dismantled in 1957, as it was too costly to maintain. It was used from 1942 as a miniature planetarium. It was built of wood and plaster and measured twenty-one feet in diameter. There was room for fifty students studying celestial navigation. This 1995 view shows the concrete base of the old conservatory and the adjoining original greenhouse. The Commandant's house is to the left. (G. Castle photo)

In recent times, the Belmont gatehouse has served as an offiice for the Colwood detachment of the RCMP, as Belmont Town Hall, and, later, as a Military Family Resource Centre. (G. Castle photo)

Cottage No. 2, where William Steers, the gardener who used to be in charge of the conservatory and greenhouse complex, lived. Latterly, this building was the military college chaplain's residence. Cottage No. 4, near the old stables, was where Jamieson lived. It is very similar in appearance. (G. Castle photo)

The Dunsmuirs are buried in the Presbyterian section of Ross Bay Cemetery. The grave marker is a polished grey granite pedestal with a cornice and pediment. There is a draped urn on top inscribed with an epitaph to Jim (Boy), who died in the sinking of the *Lusitania* in 1915. (G. Castle photo)

The former Oak Bay home of Arthur Selden and Kathleen ("Kat") Humphreys. This attractive California Spanish style home, designed by architect Ralph Berrill, was built in 1929. Landscaping was done by William Westby, whose commissions included part of the Butchart Gardens. (G. Castle photo)

Drawing room in 1995. Items to note are the original chandeliers, garlands and moulding highlighted in real gold leaf, one of two fireplaces in this room, which used to have mirrors over them, and arched doors which open on to the terrace. (G. Castle photo)

The familiar peacocks at Hatley Park did not arrive until 1965, the year before Dola, the last of the children of James and Laura Dunsmuir, died. Two pair were presented to the college by Mr. and Mrs. Fitzgerald of Penticton. (G. Castle photo)

The garden steps leading to the statue of Neptune (Greek god of the sea) in the last winter before final weeks of Royal Roads Military College. View from porte cochere of Hatley Castle looking northward to the Grant Block, built in 1942. (G. Castle photo)

The splendour falls on castle walls
  And snowy summits old in story:
The long light shakes across the lakes,
  And the wild cataract leaps in glory.
Blow, bugle, blow, set the wild echoes flying,
Blow, bugle, answer, echoes, dying, dying, dying.

"The Splendour Falls"
Alfred, Lord Tennyson
(RRMC)

Biographical Notes

Ginnie Beardsley

A freelance newspaper writer with excellent photographic skills, she has researched a number of heritage buildings and resides in Victoria.

Geoffrey Castle

After coming to Victoria from England in 1949, Geoffrey Castle worked in the land surveying field and in regional planning. He graduated from the University of Victoria and became an archivist. For some years he has devoted time and energy to encouraging heritage preservation. In 1986 he received a special Award of Merit for work in this area from the Hallmark Society. In 1994, he received the Heritage Society of British Columbia Personal Achievement Award in recognition of his impact on public awareness of Greater Victoria heritage through newspaper articles, books and lectures. He is past president of the Victoria Historical Society and chairman of the Oak Bay Heritage Foundation.

Sydney Jackman

Upon completing his secondary education in Victoria, Sydney W. Jackman went on to the University of Washington and later to Harvard University. He taught in the eastern United States and became a member of the faculty of the University of Victoria. Dr. Jackman is a member of a number of academic and learned societies and has served on the editorial boards of a number of journals, written many articles and several books. It is noteworthy that he recently donated four silver candle-sticks to Government House — they once belonged to the Dunsmuirs at Hatley Park and were among the many items auctioned after Laura Dunsmuir died in 1937.

Duncan McTavish

Here was another well-connected individual. Duncan Douglas McTavish was descended from Sir James Douglas. He was one of the five children of George Archibald McTavish, an early commodore of the Victoria Yacht Club. Duncan made insurance his career but fortunately recorded some of his early memories in and around Victoria. He lived from 1881 until 1967.

James K. Nesbitt

As the grandson of biscuit manufacturer Samuel Nesbitt who came to Victoria in 1858, the year of the gold rush, and lived at Erin Hall (burned in 1962), James Knight Nesbitt was in a good position to write about the old homes and families. He joined the *Victoria Times* as a cub reporter in 1925, and his fellow reporters referred to him as the social lion. He was also well connected in political circles and covered the provincial legislature. In 1974 he was made an honorary life member of the gallery. He preferred to be known as a Newspaperman-Historian. He did much for the preservation of Craigdarroch Castle forming a society for that purpose in 1959. Nesbitt lived until 1981 and was buried in the family plot at Ross Bay cemetery.

Derek Pethick

When he was a boy, Derek W. Pethick attended Vernon Preparatory School, of which he was to say later:

"Yet I undoubtedly acquired a few things that are not easily acquired today . . . a belief that if a thing is worth doing at all it is worth doing well; and a continuing awareness that there is no real substitute for knowledge, effort or character . . . I did receive in the end from those resolute defenders of a now vanquished order what they promised I would: a preparation for life."

He graduated from the University of British Columbia with a degree in history and later was a teacher at a private school. During the 54 years he lived in Saanich where he ran a chicken farm, Pethick wrote a number of books on British Columbia history. He also wrote plays and documentaries for the Canadian Broadcasting Corporation as well as poetry. He suffered an aneurysm in May, 1988 and died at the age of 68.

Terry Reksten

Terry Reksten was born in England, grew up in Vancouver, and was educated at the University of British Columbia and at the University of Victoria. She studied English and History and was a teacher for a while. She was a founding member and vice-president of the Hallmark Society whose concern is the preservation of historic and architectural landmarks. In 1985 she was named an honorary citizen of the City of Victoria in recognition of her writing and of her work in the field of heritage preservation. She has also served on the Victoria Heritage Advisory Committee. Among the subjects she has chosen to write about are architect F.M. Rattenbury and the Dunsmuirs.

Martin Segger

Martin Segger was born in Ipswich, England, and received his education in Western Canada. He holds degrees from the University of Victoria and the Warburg Institute, University of London. As a museologist and cultural historian, he has worked for the National Museum of Canada and the Royal British Columbia Museum. He is director of the Maltwood Art Museum and Gallery. He has been involved in the history and conservation of Canadian architecture for many years, and has written numerous books and articles. He served as chairman of the City of Victoria Heritage Advisory Committee and member of the B.C. Heritage Advisory Board, director of B.C. Heritage Trust, and governor of the Heritage Canada Foundation. More recently, Mr. Segger was a councillor for the City of Victoria.

Dorothy Stranix

When her husband, Roy, a lieutenant in the Canadian navy retired from the service they moved to Colwood. Dorothy M. Stranix wrote articles for the Highway *News-Review*, the first weekly newspaper to cover the districts of View Royal, Colwood, Glen Lake, Langford, Metchosin, Sooke and Port Renfrew. She was one of the fifteen members of the Joint Centennial Committee formed in 1966 for the area. Mrs. Stranix agreed to write the history more in the spirit of a literary adventure, but she completed the task in just one year for the 1967 celebrations of Canada's first century. She died in July, 1988.

Glossary

Adamesque — features which can be likened to a variety of graceful mouldings in the Robert Adam style, the result of his four-year stay in Italy. He and his brothers John and James lived in the 18th century in England. The Adam Style was the epitome of fashion in the 1770s.

Art Nouveau — late 19th century movement in art, architecture and design, typified by plant-like shapes such as water lilies to create a sensual style.

Arts and Crafts — a movement which began in 1867 and was associated with the design principles of William Morris. Featured traditional craftsmanship and beauty derived from nature.

Ashlar — masonry cut into square blocks but with a smooth finish resulting in quality work.

Bargeboard — board secured to the gable end of a pitched roof. Bargeboards often are carved or otherwise embellished.

Baroque — massing of structures and use of domes, projecting pediments, statuary, balustrades and pilasters.

Bay window — a window projection often the full height of the room to allow more light and to afford better viewing from inside.

Beam — a horizontal structural member of wood, steel, or concrete running transversely to support a floor or roof truss

Boudoir — French word meaning a place to sulk and relates to the private chamber of a noble woman.

Castellated — towered and with battlements like a castle.

Crenellation — another name for battlement. Incidentally, in the Middle Ages it was necessary to apply to the Crown for a licence to build a castle.

Dormer — a projection from a pitched roof forming a structure of its own. A term derived from the French verb *dormir*, to sleep.

Drop finial — an ornamental post at the apex of the gable roof with most of its length below the ridge.

Fenestration — the arrangement of the windows in the facade of a building.

Half timbering — originally a framework of half logs on a solid foundation, infilled with plaster, wattle or brickwork allowing the structure to be moved to another site. Now half timbering is a decoration to create a "mock" Tudor style. Half timbers will vary from one-inch by six-inch to two-inch by eight-inch or wider boards.

Inglenook — a niche or recess large enough to accommodate a seat and forming a part of the fireplace.

Jacobean — an architectural style relating to the time of King James I of England. It was, however, a continuation of the Elizabethan, featuring carved screens and doorways, rather exotic-looking Dutch gables and turrets, which originated in the early 17th century.

Jarrah wood — Australian close-grained heavy red wood which has not been attacked by termites or other insects.

Manor house — residence of the lord of the manor in medieval times. They dropped any defensive role by the 15th century.

Midden — an ancient garbage dump. These are of vital interest to archaeologists denoting and characterizing former native settlements.

Mock Tudor — revived Tudor style with half timbered exteriors attached to the facade. No longer an integral part of the structure.

Mullion — member of wood or stone in a window dividing two or more lights.

Newel — the central column of a spiral staircase, or a main post at the base of a stairway, or on a landing. Often elaborately carved.

Parapet — a low wall along the roof of a house.

Porte cochere — a porch designed to allow the passage of vehicles. Offers some protection from the elements when entering or leaving the house.

Quatrefoil — Gothic tracery consisting of a cluster of circles. The number of circles determines the shape and the name of the pattern.

Quoin — dressed stone on the corner of a building. A stylish architectural feature from Tudor times to the Victorian era.

Random rubble — masonry consisting of stones of varying sizes and shapes.

Scottish Baronial — 19th century Revivalist style which borrowed towers, gate-houses and battlements from medieval cantles. It was a popular style for country houses well into the 20th century. A fine example is Dunrobin Castle in Scotland.

Snail-creep — blocks of granite laid in an irregular pattern.

Stanchion — a vertical supporting member, usually of steel.

Tracery — the ornamental intersecting work in the upper part of a window. Its various forms were often emulated.

Tudor arch — a late medieval pointed arch whose shanks start with a curve and continue to the apex in a straight line.

Turret — a small and slender tower sometimes added to an existing tower.

Yacca wood — a hard wood with close grain from the south seas and used for furniture making.

Chronology

300   The Salish Indians had a settlement at Esquimalt Lagoon.

1790   Sub-lieutenant Manuel Quimper of the Spanish navy named the roadstead off the lagoon Rada de Valdes y Bazan (later Royal Roads).

1849   W.C. Grant became the first settler in the Colony of Vancouver Island. He established a sawmill at Veitch Creek, Sooke.

1850   James Douglas negotiated treaties with local Indians and purchased large amounts of land in the southern part of the colony for settlement.

1851   James Dunsmuir was born at Fort Vancouver July 8, 1851. Captain Edward E. Langford bailiff of Esquimalt Farm. Son was born (long believed to be the first white male child in the colony).

1853   Chief Justice David Cameron, brother-in-law of James Douglas, built Belmont, a house on what is now the site of Fort Rodd Hill National Historic Park.

1858   The Fraser River gold rush started and caused the population of Fort Victoria to increase from 300 to about 20,000 within six weeks, eventually easing back to about 6,000.

1860   Fisgard and Race Rocks lighthouses became the first permanent such installations on the coast.

1863   A sawmill was established on what later became Hatley Park.

1871   British Columbia entered Confederation and became Canada's sixth province.

1876   James Dunsmuir married Laura Surles of North Carolina.

1877   Robert William (Robin) born. (d. 1929). Sir James Douglas died.

1878   Birth of the Dunsmuirs' first daughter, Sarah Byrd, known as "Byrdie".

1880   Another daughter, Joan Olive White, was born but lived only to 1884.

1882   Elizabeth Maud was born to the Dunsmuirs. (d. 1962).

1884   Daughter Laura Mary ("Maye") was born. (d. 1959).

1886   A son, Alexander Lee, was born. He died the following year. The Dunsmuirs built the Esquimalt and Nanaimo Railway.

1887   A daughter, Emily Elinor, was born. (d. 1938). Jubilee of Queen Victoria.

1888   Joan Marion Dunsmuir was born. (d. 1952).

1889   Robert Dunsmuir died just before Craigdarroch Castle was completed.

1890   James and Laura had another girl, Jessie Muriel ("Moulie"). (d. 1959).

1891   Kathleen Euphemia, another daughter, was born. (d. 1941).

1892   Roland Stuart built a fine home overlooking Esquimalt Lagoon. He called it Hatley Park. The Dunsmuirs moved into their new home, "Burleith", designed by architect John Teague. It over-looked the Gorge.

1894   James ("Boy") Dunsmuir born. (d. 1915).

1895   Batteries at Fort Rodd Hill were installed. Kiel Canal opened June 21.

1900   James Dunsmuir became Premier of British Columbia.

1901   Queen Victoria died. (Dunsmuir attended King Edward VII's coronation next year.)

1903   The Dunsmuirs' last daughter, Dola Frances, was born. (d. 1966). First flight of an airplane took place.

1905   Hatley Park was destroyed by fire. Provinces of Alberta and Saskatchewan formed.

1906   Dunsmuir was appointed Lieutenant-Governor of British Columbia.

1907   Dunsmuir's yacht *Thistle* burned and sank. New yacht ordered from John Brown & Co. of the Clyde, Scotland. Named *Dolaura*, for Dola and Laura.

1908   Mrs. Joan Olive Dunsmuir, widow of Robert, died. Hatley Castle under construction.

1909   Dunsmuir resigned as Lieutenant-Governor and prepared to move to Hatley.

1911   Having disposed of his business interests, Dunsmuir took his family for a holiday in Switzerland. Amundsen reached the south pole, December 14.

1913   Perimeter wall along Sooke Road built. Landscaping under way.

1914   Onset of the First World War, August 4.

1915   "Boy" was lost when the *Lusitania* was sunk off Cork, Ireland, May 7.

1918   War ended. Armistice signed November 11.

1919   James Dunsmuir sold *Dolaura*. First direct flight over the Atlantic, June 15.

1920   While at his hunting lodge at Cowichan, James died suddenly on June 6.

1925   Sarah Byrd (Audain) died at Pau in France. Hamilton Tigers suspended and fined.

1929   Stock Market crash, October. Commander Byrd flew over the South Pole, Nov. 30.

1931   King George V sanctioned prefix "Royal" for Colwood Golf and Country Club (though not official until 1936). Great Britain proclaimed complete autonomy for Canada.

1932   Muriel (Moulie) Wingfield built "Journey's End" adjacent to the Hatley estate.

1937   Laura died August 3 at Hatley Castle

1939   Great Britain declared war on Germany, September 3. Canada did so a week later.

1940   Hatley Park estate was purchased by the Canadian Government for $75,000.

1941 Naval Officer Training Establishment officially opened at Royal Roads. Kathleen (Dunsmuir) Humphreys killed in a London air raid.

1945 Second World War ended.

1966 Dola Frances Cavendish, last surviving child of James and Laura Dunsmuir, died.

1995 Royal Roads Military College closed.

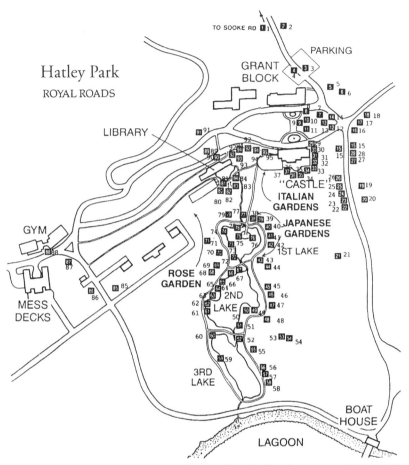

This site plan showing the location of trees identified by the Victoria Heritage Tree Society as having special significance illustrates a vital aspect of the natural heritage of 650-acre Hatley Park. (Source: Heritage Tree Book Society)

Appendix:
The Arboreal Heritage
of Hatley Park

Hatley Park was designated a Heritage Tree Area by the Victoria Horticultural Society's Heritage Tree Project, which traces its beginning to 1970. Here there are many unique and magnificent native trees, many of which can be seen from the ten kilometres of driveways and walkways through the gardens.

On passing through the entrance to the estate, the visitor will notice the **blue Atlas cedar** (1), on the right, and the **native Douglas fir** (2) on the left. At the car park there are shore pines (3), a **Japanese black pine** (4), and lower down on the left side of the entrance roads there are a **bigleaf maple** (5), **grand fir** and Douglas fir (6).

Below the car park, the road on the right leads to the Neptune steps and a Norway maple (7). Flanking the steps are two **Atlas cedars** (8) from North Africa. On both sides of the steps are "mop-head" **black locusts** (9). On the lawn on either side are purple-leaved **flowering plums** (**10**). At the foot of the steps, there are large **copper** and **purple beech** trees (11). After turning left onto the roadway, there are two large, conical **Lawson cypress** trees with branches touching the lawn (12). This tree, together with its many variations, comes from southern Oregon and northern California. In the lawn, to the left, there is a large **arbutus** (13). Significantly, this is Canada's only native broad-leaved evergreen tree. Further on the left, there is a pink flowering **eastern dogwood** (14).

Red-flowering **horse-chestnuts** (15) may be seen on both sides of the roadway at the intersection with Beach Road, which leads to Esquimalt lagoon. On the left is a towering **giant sequoia** (16) which is native to Kings Canyon, California. Next is a **Norway spruce** (17) and then a row of **lindens** (18). Continuing down the road, four **Japanese black pine** trees may be seen (19) and a **mountain ash** (20), which, in season, is heavy with clusters of red fruit. There is a grand **horse chestnut** (21) on the Castle side of Beach Road, at the parade ground, and a very large **London plane** (22) with its characteristic flaking bark and maple-like leaves. Also here is one of the largest **pin oaks** in Victoria (23). The nearby **Spanish chestnut** is noteworthy; it is a true chestnut with edible nuts. Continuing back toward the castle, there are several **tulip trees** (25), which have tulip-like flowers in early summer, and a pink-flowering **English hawthorn** (26). On the right, there is a curious-looking **monkey-puzzle tree** from Chili (27), which is a female tree, producing heavy, pod-like cones. Next is a **juniper** (28). Across the lawn, adjacent to the northeasterly corner of the castle, is a **sweet gum** (29) with a distinctive aromatic leaf when it is crushed. Near this tree is a wide-spreading **English yew** (30).

In the *Italian Garden*, where the plants include clematis, climbing roses, phlox, wisteria, delphiniums, and chrysanthemums, there are columnar **Irish yews** (31) as well as a large **linden** (32). At the end of the wall is a large **purple beech** (33) and a **Norway maple** (35), directly below the castle.

The **sycamore maple** (36), across from the gate of the Italian Garden, is a striking tree with heavy fruiting, and one of the larger ones in the Greater Victoria area. Nearby is a **silver maple** (37).

The *Japanese Garden* is enclosed with a deer fence. There are three lakes created from springs on the property. Left of the fence, going towards the lagoon, there is a **copper beach** tree (38), and a grand **scarlet oak** (39), a graceful **deodar cedar** (40), contrasting with a **golden English holly** (41). There are three more **copper beech** trees (42), a **European ash** with black buds (43), another **linden** (44), a **red oak** (45), a **weeping ash** (46), and a columnar **English oak** (47).

There is an **Oregon ash** (48) near the bottom of the second lake. It is smaller than the nearby **European ash** (49). A native **Sitka spruce** (50), by the edge of the lake, is capable of growing to immense size on the Queen Charlotte Islands. Nearby is a **Japanese katsura** tree (51) with a distinctive leaf and bark yielding beautiful colours in the autumn. The Japanese garden includes cherry trees, Japanese umbrella pines, copper beeches, Western red cedars and rhododendrons. Fish ladders connect the three lakes with the lagoon. Near the little bridge, there is a spring-flowering magnolia.

At the lower lake is an *English Natural Garden*. There is a **Spanish chestnut** (52) on the lake side of the path, and in the field there are two **shore pines** (53), and a **Norway maple** (54). There is also a fine **vine maple** (55), opposite, which is uncommon on Vancouver Island. There are two **English oaks** (56), and further along the path is a native western **red cedar** (57). There is a **London plane** tree near the end of the lake (58).

Along the return path on the opposite side of the lake, southwest **elms** (59) of various species. At the top end of this lake, there are three **lindens** (60), and there are several **tulip trees** (61) on either side of the path at the second lake. There is a **cut-leaf birch** by the water's edge at the head of the lake, where there is also a **golden Lawson cypress** (65) as well as a **European ash, copper beech** and a **silver maple**. Among these is the uncommon **Judas tree** (66), which has deep pink pea-like flowers in early spring. Along the cross path, there are three **Norway maples** (67). On the left, southwest of the iron fence and path, is a columnar **English oak** (68), and a **European ash** (69). Along the path is a **Colorado blue spruce** (70) and another **European linden** tree (71).

At the upper edge of the lake, there are several **flowering cherry trees** (72) and **flower crabapples** (73). Half way up the lake is a fine **halfmoon maple** (74). On Tortoise (Midshipman's) Island, there is a **Japanese white pine** (75). (The tortoise represents longevity). On the island, with the teahouse, there is an **Atlas cedar** (76).

At the head of the lake, along the path are **a false cypress** (77); a saucer **magnolia** (78); two forms of **threadleaf Japanese maples** (79); another **full moon maple,** and four splendid rare **Japanese umbrella pines** (80). Also in the vicinity are a form of **weeping beech** (81); a striking golden pyramidal **false cypress** (82) and, forming a backdrop for this area of the garden, are a **Western red cedar** (83) and some **big-leaf maples** (84).

In the greenhouse area, there is a **white mulberry**. It is probably the largest in Canada and always fruits heavily. Growing into the greenhouse, through a window, is a "Black Hamburg" **grapevine** which started growing around 1910 when it was taken as a cutting from a 200-year-old vine at Hampton Court Palace in England. The path above the greenhouse area is lined with **black walnuts** (87) and a **southern catalpa** (88).

It is interesting to note that nearby there are remnants of an orchard which predates the Dunsmuir ownership, planted as part of the Hudson's Bay Company Colwood Farm.

Along the path in the direction of the library building, there is an **American chestnut** on the left (89). This eastern tree was almost completely destroyed by a blight some years ago. A **Giant sequoia** (90) of the weeping kind leans over the library. Nearby are tall, slender **black locusts** (91). These once lined the loop road from the eastern to the western entrance of the estate. **Red maples** line the lower road to the castle (92). There are two variegated **Manitoba maples** or **box-elders** (93) in the lawn below the road. Nearer the castle, there is a **pin oak** and also a **white birch.**

Reproduced by kind permission of the Heritage Tree Book Society.

BIBLIOGRAPHY

Audain, James. *Alex Dunsmuir's Dilemma*. Victoria: Sunnylane, 1964.

Audain, James. *From Coalmine to Castle*. New York: Pageant Press, 1955.

Bingham, Janet. *Samuel Maclure, Architect*. Ganges: Horsdal and Schubart, 1985.

Castle, Geoffrey and King, Barry F. *Victoria Landmarks*. Victoria: Geoffrey Castle and Barry King, 1985.

City of Colwood. *Heritage Inventory*. Colwood: City of Colwood, 1988.

Coleman, Terry. *The Liners*. Penguin: 1985.

Cotton, Peter. *Vice Regal Mansions of British Columbia*. Victoria: Elgin Publications, 1981.

Crows, Philip A. *The Intelligent Traveller's Guide to Historic Ireland*. Dublin: Gill and Macmillan, 1990.

Goodacre, Richard. *Dunsmuir's Dream*. Victoria: Porcepic Books, 1991.

Gregson, Harry. *A History of Victoria: 1842-1970*. Vancouver: J.J. Douglas, 1977.

Howay, F.W. and Scholefield, E.O.S. *British Columbia From the Earliest Times to the Present*. Vancouver: Clarke, 1914. 4 vols.

Jackman, S.W. *The Men at Cary Castle*. Victoria: Morriss, 1972.

Jenner, Michael. *The Architectural Heritage of Britain and Ireland*. Harmondsworth: Penguin, 1993.

Lugrin, N. de Bertrand. *The Pioneer Women of Vancouver Island*. Victoria: The Women's Canadian Club of Victoria, 1928.

Mills, John. *Up in the Clouds, Gentlemen Please*. Harmondsworth: Penguin, 1981.

Neill, J.W. ed. *Trees of Greater Victoria: A Heritage*. Victoria: Heritage Tree Book Society, 1988.

Pethick, Derek. *Men of British Columbia*. Saanichton: Hancock House, 1975.

Pethick, Derek. *Summer of Promise*. Victoria: Sono Nis, 1980.

Reksten, Terry. *A Century of Sailing 1892–1992.* Victoria: Orca, 1992.

Reksten, Terry. *The Dunsmuir Saga.* Vancouver: Douglas and McIntyre, 1991.

Segger, Martin. *The Buildings of Samuel Maclure.* Victoria, Sono Nis, 1986.

Smith, Dorothy Blakey, ed. *The Reminiscences of Dr. John Sebastian Helmcken.* Vancouver: U.B.C. Press, 1975.

Stranix, Dorothy. *Notes and Quotes.* Victoria: Joint Centennial Committee for Colwood, Langford, Metchosin, Happy Valley and Glen Lake, 1967.

Walbran, John T. *British Columbia Coast Names 1592–1906.* Vancouver: J.J. Douglas, 1971. Reprinted.

Sources

Collections:

British Columbia Archives and Records Service (BCARS)
Craigdarroch Castle Archives (CCA)
Esquimalt Archives (EA)
Esquimalt Naval Museum and Archives (ENM)
Royal Roads Military College Library and Archives (RRMC)
Victoria Public Library (VPL)

Newspapers:

Goldstream Gazette
Highway News Review
Juan de Fuca News Review
Times-Colonist
Victoria Daily Colonist

Index